Live Life Like a Kung Fu Master

William Moy
Paul Volponi

Skyhorse Publishing

For my father, who taught me the beauty of simplicity
and my mother, who showed me the heart of giving.
—William Moy

Copyright © 2025 by William Moy and Paul Volponi

All rights reserved. No part of this book may be reproduced in any manner without the express written consent of the publisher, except in the case of brief excerpts in critical reviews or articles. All inquiries should be addressed to Skyhorse Publishing, 307 West 36th Street, 11th Floor, New York, NY 10018.

Skyhorse Publishing books may be purchased in bulk at special discounts for sales promotion, corporate gifts, fund-raising, or educational purposes. Special editions can also be created to specifications. For details, contact the Special Sales Department, Skyhorse Publishing, 307 West 36th Street, 11th Floor, New York, NY 10018 or info@skyhorsepublishing.com.

Skyhorse® and Skyhorse Publishing® are registered trademarks of Skyhorse Publishing, Inc.®, a Delaware corporation.

Visit our website at www.skyhorsepublishing.com.

10 9 8 7 6 5 4 3 2 1

Library of Congress Cataloging-in-Publication Data is available on file.

Jacket design by David Ter-Avanesyan
Cover photo by Anthony Lucic
Interior sketches courtesy of William Moy
Photographs supplied by the author

Print ISBN: 978-1-5107-8125-2
Ebook ISBN: 978-1-5107-8126-9

Printed in the United States of America

"If someone asks you what is Kung Fu, the answer is: Kung Fu is life. So then, another question: What is life? . . . Life is everything."
—Moy Yat (1938–2001)

CONTENTS

Introduction   vii
A Welcome from Sifu William Moy

Chapter One: The Shortest Route (Center Line Theory)   1
*The best way from Point A to Point B, in self-defense
and living our lives*

Chapter Two: The Language of Kung Fu   11
Broadening horizons through knowledge

Chapter Three: The Little Beginning Idea (*Siu Nim Tao*)   27
A Kung Fu alphabet/ Building words then sentences to define us

Chapter Four: Why a Kung Fu Family?   39
Passing it forward/Finding a web of support

Chapter Five: Structure and Position   53
The power of keeping yourself together

Chapter Six: Maintaining Balance and Finding a Horse   63
Bending but never breaking

Chapter Seven: Distance Awareness and Angles   73
Martialing distance for success

Chapter Eight: A "System" of Kung Fu   87
Moving ahead in your life through diligence

Chapter Nine: Chi Sau and Sticking Energy 99
Controlling the central aspects of life

Chapter Ten: Relaxation over Tenseness 111
Feeling more and stressing less

Chapter Eleven: Redirecting External Forces 123
We don't need to absorb the full brunt of others

Chapter Twelve: Facing and Helping Hands 133
Keeping sight of your goals and options

Chapter Thirteen: Body Unity (*Chum Kiu*) 145
The power of motion/Never becoming stagnant

Chapter Fourteen: Creating Leverage for Ourselves 155
Gathering strength through internal mechanics

Chapter Fifteen: A Model of Efficiency 165
A life with less wasted time and effort

Chapter Sixteen: Ego Is the Enemy 177
Maintaining proper perspective on ourselves and others

Chapter Seventeen: Recovering from the Unexpected (*Biu Jee*) 189
An evolving plan for every bump in the road

Chapter Eighteen: Sidestepping Potential Conflict/Accepting the
Unavoidable 199
On your timetable, even when your hand is forced

Chapter Nineteen: The Wooden Dummy and Beyond 211
Building upon and redefining our skills

Chapter Twenty: Taking Your *Good Kung Fu* into Tomorrow 221
New knowledge, new attitude, new day

Departing Thoughts: On Car Rides 227
Special Thanks 229

INTRODUCTION

HELLO. MY NAME IS William Moy and many people consider me to be a master of Kung Fu. Being called a "master" is always interesting for me to hear and fully digest. That's because Kung Fu is an art at which you never stop learning and growing as an individual. Though I've been training and teaching Kung Fu for more than four decades, I'm still advancing on my own path toward a deeper understanding of the art, the world around me . . . and myself.

I initially learned Kung Fu from my father, Moy Yat, who in turn was instructed by his teacher, or *sifu*, Ip Man, one of the most famous Chinese martial artists of the last century. Perhaps you recognize Ip Man's name from the multiple blockbuster films made about his life. Or maybe you know of him through his most famous student, Bruce Lee, who was an older Kung Fu brother, or *si hing*, to my father.

Before I go any further, allow me to pause for a moment in order to embrace *you* as my Kung Fu brethren as well. Whether you know it or not, on some level you have been a practitioner of Kung Fu since your earliest years. How so? Well, if I called to you from across a semi-crowded room to let you know that I had just

Live Life Like a Kung Fu Master

found your wallet on the floor, you would probably begin by taking a step in my direction with an "Oh, thank you" already forming on your lips. But in that instant, if I took you by surprise and tossed you the wallet from several feet away instead of directly handing it to you, your *natural Kung Fu* reactions would take over. You see, the term "Kung Fu" literally translates to "time and effort equals a skill." Catching things is something you've practiced your entire life. Your brain would also be simultaneously processing that I've tossed you a wallet and not a heavy stone. Visually, you would observe the arc of my toss. Without thinking, you would adjust the position of your hands and posture to align yourself with the wallet in midair, all the while accounting spatially for the people and objects around you.

Congratulations. That's a good amount of Kung Fu that you already possess!

My goal in writing this book is to increase your overall knowledge of Kung Fu, giving you the opportunity to hone and enhance the natural skills you have while also opening the door to new ideas and techniques. This knowledge will not only serve you in a basic self-defense scenario, but also in your everyday dealings with your family, friends, business associates, and even strangers you encounter on the street. Chinese culture highly values people who possess *good Kung Fu*, but that phrase applies more to individuals who can control their lives and relationships while treating others respectfully than it does to those who are skilled fighters.

There are several hundred styles and systems of Kung Fu. My expertise is in a system known as Wing Chun Kung Fu, which is the most popular in the world today, practiced by nearly three million people. Legend has it that Wing Chun is the only martial art invented by a woman (Ng Mui, a member of the Shaolin Temple). Correspondingly, it relies more on physics—distance,

Introduction

balance, and angles—than brute strength. It is a system that preaches simplicity and straightforward efficiency through its use of a center line theory, traveling the shortest distance between two points.

This resulting efficiency has made me an accomplished multitasker in my busy life as a sifu, son, husband, father of two, and responsible member of my community. And I'm confident that an increased understanding of the art will translate into prosperous outcomes in your life as well.

Of course, my Kung Fu won't be the same as yours. Remember that this is an individual art which varies from practitioner to practitioner depending on their personality, attributes, and physical strengths and weaknesses. My father was a huge proponent of allowing his students to find their own Kung Fu, and I believe the same.

Along with multi-award-winning, bestselling author Paul Volponi, a longtime student of the art and disciple of mine, I will introduce you to the fundamental concepts of Kung Fu. These concepts, as they apply to both self-defense and your daily challenges, will be accompanied by personal anecdotes and life examples provided by me and a wide spectrum of valued contributors—all in an effort to bring you closer to a life made better by Kung Fu. Naturally, we'll examine aspects of the Chinese culture, which gave birth to, and influences the art so profoundly. Throughout the chapters, which contain simple drawings of mine to illustrate certain concepts. I will also direct you to approximately twenty YouTube videos that I have created especially for the readers of this book, allowing you to visualize many of the discussed techniques and forms.

My goal for *Live Life Like a Kung Fu Master* is not to teach you how to fight, although I believe you will learn about techniques that may safeguard you from the potential negative and sometimes dangerous situations that we all encounter from time to time.

Wing Chun is a self-correcting martial art. That means that as you advance in your knowledge of the system, you will begin to make subtle adjustments to improve your Kung Fu. In essence, you will eventually assume the job of being your own sifu. Because, after all, who understands your journey better than you?

But for now, I relish the role of being your teacher, and you may refer to me as Sifu William.

My father, Moy Yat, once told me that "Kung Fu gets into your bones and reflects on everything you do." Over many years, I have found that statement to be remarkably true. I hope that, one day, you too will experience that kind of bonding with the art. And that you will truly learn to live your life like a Kung Fu master.

Note: Though my specific Kung Fu lineage actually refers to the art as "Ving Tsun," throughout this text I will use the more commonly accepted phrase "Wing Chun," so as not to confuse newcomers.

CHAPTER ONE

The Shortest Route (Center Line Theory)

The shortest distance between two points is a straight line.

—Archimedes, Greek mathematician and physicist

WE ALL HAVE THINGS that we consider to be *central* to our lives: family, friends, our home, our profession, passions, and beliefs. Because they are so important to us, we carefully nurture and diligently protect them. Similarly, Kung Fu practitioners physically protect their center with the same fervor.

PHYSICAL ATTRIBUTES

In the art of Wing Chun Kung Fu, we consider our center line to be our most valuable asset. Clearly, most of our vital organs are positioned there, and so are those belonging to our opponent. That's why we put so much emphasis on simultaneously defending our center line while also using it to attack our opponent's center. *Simultaneously?* Yes, because our attack actually occupies the center line, affording a substantial defense as well.

Exactly how do we define the center line? It's an imaginary line drawn vertically down the center of the body, connecting the eyes, nose, throat, abdomen, groin, and knees. We position our hands one behind the other (one forward, one back) upon the center line, with them extended out in front of us and our elbows protecting our body. It's a basic "on guard" position that we refer to as *jong sau*.

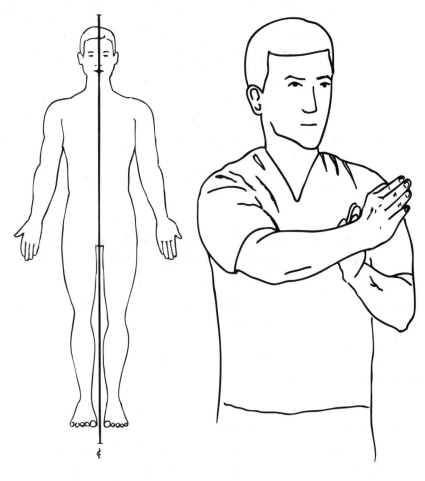

The Shortest Route (Center Line Theory)

In a split second, however, our guard can transform into an attack. Open hands can turn into fists, churning one over top the other like powerful pistons delivering strikes, with neither hand ever leaving the center line. The straight punch (*yat je jung choi*) possesses a lightning-quick delivery—so much so that multiple strikes can seemingly blend into a singular unceasing blow.

For a visual demonstration, go to YouTube and search: "Live Life Like a Kung Fu Master—William Moy, Chain Punches."

Naturally, there is another important aspect as to why the center line is so cherished. Any mathematician or engineer will assure you that the shortest distance between two points is a straight line (just ask Archimedes). That's why we fire our strikes down the center. If we can arrive at our targeted destination a fraction of a second before a punch aimed at us that has a hook or a bend to it (hence traveling a further distance), we can interrupt our opponent's attack, often completely short-circuiting their power mid-punch while also negatively affecting their balance.

One of the classic maneuvers in the annals of military warfare is the penetration of the opposing force's center. This is accomplished by either exploiting a natural gap or creating one in the opposition's line of defense, allowing for a strike directly into the center of their command base. Comparatively, a Kung Fu practitioner might create an opening in the opponent's guard by separating and then controlling their limbs in order to successfully to attack along the center line.

FROM MY LIFE: INDIRECTLY DIRECT

Throughout my training, my father showed me how to find the center line in two of my life's main pursuits: Kung Fu and art.

Live Life Like a Kung Fu Master

As a young child, I would watch my father paint and draw. I was fascinated by the process of creating something out of nothing, especially something beautiful. I was the middle child of three, with an older and younger sister flanking me on either side. But of that trio of children, the need for artistic expression burned inside of me the strongest. I remember taking out paper and working beside my father, drawing things such as rudimentary landscapes, birds, and trees. Neither of my parents ever pushed me to participate. Instead, it came to me naturally, with my father simply showing me the way by example.

I was probably six years old when he first handed me a sheet of rice paper on which to work. Even back then, I understood that this paper was costly and not something to be treated wastefully. I'm sure it felt satisfying for my father to have that type of respect and confidence in my budding ability as an artist.

Coming to Kung Fu, however, was quite a different endeavor. My journey had several minor bends to it. In the absence of an available babysitter, I often accompanied my father to his Kung Fu school, where I would mostly sit on the side and entertain myself. Given the choice, however, I would have rather been hanging out with my friends, playing touch football, basketball, or street hockey. It was an easy decision for me. After all, the school was mostly filled with sweaty men and women in their early twenties and beyond. Not exactly a paradise of good times for an eight year old.

Then I met Rex, who was my father's first US student to open a branch school bearing the Moy Yat name and plum flower emblem. Rex had already moved to Tallahassee, Florida, to start both a family and his own Kung Fu school. He came back to New York every six months or so to continue his training with my father. And whenever he did, my father would invite him to stay at our apartment. On those visits, Rex took on the role of the big brother I never had. I looked up to him, and he decided to teach

[4]

The Shortest Route (Center Line Theory)

me some Kung Fu, even before my father—just an eyedropper full.

That summer, Rex invited me down to Florida to stay with his family and meet his two boys. I was excited to go, and my parents allowed me to fly down alone. I remember my mom was really anxious about me taking the trip by myself, but my father said, "Traveling alone will help him to mature."

I had a great time in Florida. Coming from New York City, Tallahassee seemed like the wilderness to me. I went fishing with Rex's kids, swam in a lake, and played in the countryside. Rex also took us to his Kung Fu school and introduced me to his students as Moy Yat's son. That entire afternoon, those teens and adults were coming up to me, asking questions about Kung Fu, and what it was like to be the son of a grandmaster. For the first time, I was embarrassed by how little I actually knew of the art.

When the trip was over and I returned home, one of the first things I told my father was that I wanted to attend his class regularly and begin to really learn Kung Fu. I remember my father nodding his head, giving me a satisfied smile in response. And as I look back on my memory of that smile today, as a father with children of my own, I have come to believe that allowing me to go on that trip was my father's way of providing a straightforward path toward what would become another true passion of mine.

> *At the center of your being you have the answer. You know who you are and you know what you want.*
> —Lao Tzu, Chinese philosopher

STRAIGHT AND TRUE?

The GPS in our cars and phones consistently offer us the shortest route between a starting point and a destination. It will even take into account toll roads and bridges, leaving us a choice between the shortest route in distance/time and the most economical route in terms of expense.

However, in our daily dealings with others—friends, family partners, coworkers—we must serve as our own internal GPS, choosing which route to take in our many and varied relationships. Will we be straight to the pointwith others, or not? And what will a deviation in directness ultimately cost us in terms of time and trust?

Transferring Kung Fu's center line theory into our communications and relationships can provide more clarity and, in the long run, give our relationships a stronger, more stable foundation. Consider these common situations: We often shade our true feelings, thoughts, and opinions—especially when dealing with someone who doesn't view a specific situation the same way in which we do. We may be clouding things out of politeness, trying not to hurt someone's feelings. Or perhaps we're the ones desiring a connection to a group or individual, and believe that our difference of opinion will cause friction and, perhaps, rejection.

It can take weeks, months, or sadly even years for the truth between people to finally surface, providing a clearer understanding of one another. Beating around the bush about your true feelings is rarely a good idea, with the less-than-optimal Kung Fu–related word being *around*. Instead, try to be straight to the point with others from the start. Though the initial conversation may be uncomfortable, the end result will most likely be less wasted effort and frustration.

Miscommunication can be a much greater hindrance to building a good relationship than expressing the truth.

NATURAL KUNG FU: LEARNING/TEACHING WITH A PURPOSE

Consider the game of tic-tac-toe. From a very young age, we learn that taking the center square as our first move leaves the opposing

The Shortest Route (Center Line Theory)

player with more opportunities to make a mistake, allowing us to ultimately increase the likelihood of emerging victorious.As we advance in our ability to strategize, we begin to play chess and quickly come to realize that controlling the center of a chessboard with our pawns is a premium. There is an axiom in chess that states, "Controlling the center is to control the game."

For nearly two decades, chess coach Russ Makofsky has been instructing NYC public school students about the value of chess and what its mastery can bring to their future lives.

"Chess is like life," said Coach Russ. "It's a game of real estate and you want to control its most valued neighborhood—the board's center—because that will ultimately put you on a path to success. Most of the game's established openings focus on that theory."

Controlling those vitally important center squares improves both your offense and defense, giving your pieces more room to maneuver and, therefore, creating more opportunities and options down the line. You can also relocate your pieces more quickly through the center of the board, facilitating faster and easier defense and attack maneuvers to either side. Sounds a lot like Kung Fu, especially in the notion that occupying the center can cramp your opponent's movements.

"I teach my students the saying, 'A knight on the rim is dim.' Understand this: a knight stuck in the corner can control just two squares, and that same piece positioned on the side, four squares. But a knight in the center of the board can actually control eight squares," noted Coach Russ. "Through the study of chess, we're trying to create an environment that fosters the pursuit of excellence."

Coach Russ is also passionate about his work with an organization called The Gift of Chess. The organization's goal is to eventually give away one million chess boards worldwide.

"So many people play via their computer now. We're trying to bring neighborhoods together by encouraging people to play face to face in parks and other spaces, in order to meet and learn about one another," said Coach Russ.

PAUL'S PERSPECTIVE: MAKING ALL THE DIFFERENCE

"Throughout our chapters, coauthor Paul Volponi will weigh in with his thoughts and perspective, relating Kung Fu to both his personal experiences and our daily lives."

Over my long career as a writer and an educator, I have often had the pleasure of discussing Robert Frost's masterful narrative poem, *The Road Not Taken*. For those of you who might need a quick refresher, the poem famously begins with the lines:

Two roads diverged in a yellow wood,
And sorry I could not travel both
And be one traveler . . .

The narrator is standing at the crossroads, a fork in the road, presumably being presented with a choice of either going to the right or the left. I suppose that at least once in an English class somewhere a student stood up and said, "You know, I think Mr. Frost could use a good lesson in efficiency. He hasn't given us the opportunity to continue on straight down the center, to arrive at our destination quicker." I don't know what the teacher overseeing that classroom might have said in return to such an observant student. Maybe praise. Maybe a dismissive or amused look before calling on the next hand to be raised. But I'm fairly confident that particular student, who already sees the value of a straight-line journey, would enjoy a more detailed introduction to Kung Fu. So if you know such a student, whether they be a tween, teen, or

The Shortest Route (Center Line Theory)

adult with children of their own, pass this book along to them when you've finished reading. After all, to paraphrase Robert Frost, it could possibly become part of making *all the difference* in their life, as lots of books have a way of doing.

LIFE APPLICATIONS

- It's raining hard today, so you decide to take the local instead of the express bus, which actually makes several fewer stops. But unlike the local, the express bus veers some six blocks south of your intended final destination.
- A catcher crouched behind home plate keeps a wary eye on the runner at first base, knowing that runner is likely to attempt to steal second base. So the catcher gives the pitcher a sign to throw a fastball instead of a curve, realizing the straighter pitch without a bend will get to home plate quicker, providing the catcher a better opportunity to thwart the potential theft.
- At the start of an exam with unequally weighted questions you decide to go directly to the final section where the problems are worth three times the points, as a safeguard against running out of time.
- You attend a show inside a theater that has general admission seating, so you can choose any open seat. You decide to sit on the center aisle. Why? Not only will the most important part of the show undoubtedly take place at center stage, where you should have a perfectly aligned view, but in an emergency you can quickly access the aisle, affording you a straight line journey to the appropriate exit.

Nature is an infinite sphere of which the center is everywhere and the circumference nowhere.
—Blaise Pascal, French mathematician and physicist.

THE SHAOLIN TEMPLE AND KUNG FU

Kung Fu has a history dating back centuries, even though its transplanted roots in the US are just several decades old. Nearly every style and system of Kung Fu can trace its lineage back to the Shaolin Temple, located in the mountains of northern China's Henan Province. The legendary temple is recognized as both the birthplace of Chan Buddhism and the cradle of Kung Fu. It is where the monks of Shaolin have dedicated themselves to the study and mastery of martial arts in devotion to the Buddha.

As far back as the sixth century, there are records of Shaolin monks using their martial skills to defend the Temple in fighting off bandits who were intent on overrunning its grounds. Though these martial skills were long taught in secrecy behind closed doors, other forms of culture, such as Chinese opera, recognized these arts through plotlines, openly celebrating their existence.

The twentieth century, however, brought about a change in the accessibility of Chinese martial arts to a significantly broader audience, as they were promoted by the government as a form of national pride.

With the coming to power of the People's Republic of China in 1949, many martial arts masters escaped communist rule, immigrating to Hong Kong, other Asian countries and the West. This new wave of masters began teaching traditional arts to non-Chinese students, with the many benefits of Kung Fu ultimately finding a place in the hearts of diverse practitioners around the world.

CHAPTER TWO

THE LANGUAGE OF KUNG FU

Learning another language is not only learning different words for the same things, but learning another way to think about things.

—Flora Lewis, award-winning journalist

COMMUNICATION IS OUR MOST vital tool in navigating the world around us—be it the spoken word, our overall body language, or a clearly defined glance—connecting our thoughts to others.

PHYSICAL ATTRIBUTES

Speaking Kung Fu can take many forms. Of course, the art has its own language, its glossary of terms—most of which find their roots in Cantonese. This is an important reference point for practitioners around the world to compare and contrastideas and theories concerning the art. It is also the best way for a sifu to ground their students in the basics so they can effectively communicate with both their teacher and classmates. But the language of Kung Fu isn't confined to a list of vocabulary words. The art can also be communicated through a practitioner's body language.

For example, if a Kung Fu practitioner is approached in the street by a stranger, you may find their suddenly aligned hands held slightly out in front of them occupying the center line in a very relaxed manner. Perhaps only another practitioner of the art would read this as a subtle on guard or safety position. However, if that stranger in the street approached the same practitioner in an over-the-top, aggressive manner, the *spoken* response would almost certainly be much different. You would view nothing subtle in the classic *jong sau* position, which can appear quite threatening with both arms fully extended in "knife-hand" positions.

The Language of Kung Fu

In many martial arts schools, belts are worn to identify a student's rank, ranging from white (for novices) all the way up to black, often delineated further by stripes for experienced practitioners. Neither I nor my father, though, ever saw the need for our students to be designated in this manner. In place of belts, we used three distinctly colored shirts: white, green, and red. Those shirts served the purpose of letting other students know which exercises their classmates were working on for when they were paired up to train.

But, in reality, it wouldn't take one practitioner long—probably no more than a few seconds—to understand their partner's skill level. By putting your hands into the hands of one of your classmates and *playing* Kung Fu (we use the term "playing" to separate training from sparring or fighting, and to emphasize the joy in this type of one-on-one communication), you listen to the language they're speaking through their actions and responses, tenseness and relaxation, and understand where they are in learning the system. That's speaking the language of Kung Fu at its best, and is often referred to as "talking hands."

A TRIO OF TECHNIQUES

Here I'm going to introduce you to a trio of key Kung Fu terms that describe foundational techniques with which every beginner needs to become familiar. They are *tan sau*, *fuk sau*, and *bong sau*.

Tan Sau

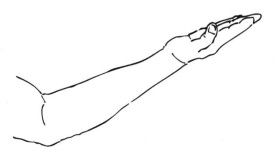

The hand is fully supinated, with the palm facing up and the fingers pointing toward what would be an opponent's throat-level area. The arm is placed in front of the practitioner's sternum with the elbow anchored approximately a fist and a half (in length) away from the body, positioned on the imaginary center line. This technique is superior for facilitating outward/upward movement with the energy flowing in the direction of the fingertips.

Fuk Sau

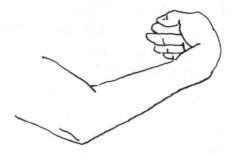

The hand is pronated with the palm facing downward or inward. Again, the arm is placed in front of the practitioner's sternum with the elbow anchored approximately a fist and a half (in length) away from the body, positioned on the imaginary center line. This technique is used for generating inward or downward movement. It is often used to control, block, or cover strikes aimed below the head area.

Bong Sau

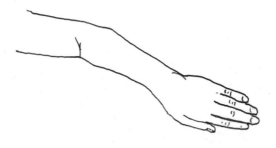

With your wrist on the imaginary center line and your hand facing toward the opponent's chin, the elbow, which is slightly above the wrist, is up and level with your shoulder. It very much resembles a bird's broken wing, and is the "wing hand" of Wing Chun Kung Fu. This technique is designed to facilitate up and outward movement. It is used to deflect straight attacks, while having a secondary ability to create openings.

CHECKING YOURSELF

In the physical absence of a sifu, or even a mirror, you can check whether or not you are performing these techniques correctly. How so? Start with a *tan sau*. If positioned correctly, you can change to either a *fuk sau* or *bong sau* without adjustingthe position occupied by the wrist. As long as the wrist is on the center line and the elbow is directly behind it (off to its side in bong sau), you're perfect. All three techniques can be checked in this manner, easily and swiftly transforming from one to another.

> **For a visual demonstration, go to YouTube and search: "Live Life Like a Kung Fu Master—William Moy, Tan Sau, Fuk Sau, Bong Sau (meld)."**

A FEEL FOR CANTONESE

You have probably noticed that all three techniques I've presented end with the word *sau*, which means "hand" in Cantonese. *Tan sau* translates as the receiving or dispersing hand. *Fuk Sau* translates as the hand that can tame an incoming force. *Bong sau* translates as a wing-arched hand, perfectly describing its structure.

Traditionally, during our class warmups, students count out their repetition of exercises, such as punching and kicking drills, using the numbers one through eight in Cantonese. The numbers

Live Life Like a Kung Fu Master

translate as *yat* (one), *yee* (two), *sa(m)* (three), *say* (four), *mm* (five), *lok* (six), *chat* (seven), and *bah(t)* (eight). It's a great way to practice the language and have it become second nature.

FROM MY LIFE: ONLY AS YOU CAN

After immigrating to the US, my father would make annual trips back to Hong Kong to visit with family and friends. This included time spent with his Kung Fu family as well. In this regard, his two most important stops were to the grave of Ip Man—paying respect to the person who had assumed the role of his Kung Fu father—and to the local athletic association where he had trained along with his many classmates.

Upon returning from one particular trip, I remember my father recounting the story of meeting up with one of his classmates who had become a sifu, teaching a large number of local students. In bragging a bit about one of his students, that sifu told my father to keep his eyes open for someone playing the art's first form, *Siu Nim Tao* (this text's succeeding chapter focuses on its importance) with an elegant and exaggerated flip of the hand. That struck a chord in my father's memory, recalling that this had been his classmate's signature move while doing that form. Graciously, my father said that he would look for such a student and treat him as his own. But in the back of my father's mind, he wholeheartedly disagreed with the premise of passing down such a signature. And that had to do with the necessity of each student speaking the language, or in this instance, the body language of Kung Fu, using their own natural voice.

My father firmly believed that there were, in actuality, two distinct systems of Kung Fu. The first system is the one that has remained virtually unchanged for generations. That would consist of the order of forms, exercises, and techniques teachers use to introduce, grow, and, ultimately, refine the talents of their

[16]

students. The second system, however, is less formal and much more personal. That one is reflective in how the Kung Fu looks and feels in its application by each individual practitioner. Those movements will be substantially influenced by the student's physical and mental makeup. Copying others without deviation is not a diagram to developing good Kung Fu, even if the person to be copied is your own sifu.

For example, Ip Man, because of his small stature, played his *tan sau* rather high. But my father, who was over six feet tall, didn't need to do that. Despite learning from a martial arts legend, my father never tried to emulate how his sifu played that technique. That's because it would have been a mistake, translating to a technique that would have proved to be less effective. Instead, my father spoke the language of Kung Fu as it naturally flowed through him and no one else. This is something that I have recognized in myself in developing my own Kung Fu, as my father was slightly taller and lankier than me.

And as my student, I gladly pass this story and its lesson onto you: Be a true reflection of yourself in all of your communications with others.

> *Language exerts hidden power, like the moon on the tides.*
> —Rita Mae Brown, novelist and civil rights activist

MULTIPLE KUNG FU VOICES

We all have experience communicating with others using our eyes and facial expressions to convey our immediate feelings. Often a stern or disappointed look in the direction of children or younger siblings can take the place of a wordy lecture they may have already heard numerous times. That same type of silent expression can also make it clear to a stranger with whom we have become wary that we are confident in our ability to defend

Live Life Like a Kung Fu Master

ourselves. Posture can be an important co-contributor in getting across that message as well. Always stand tall and confidently, even in the shadow of uncertainty.

Perhaps you've chosen not to make direct eye contact with someone on the street who appears ready to explode at the slightest personal encounter. That's actually a good bit of natural Kung Fu on your part, something you've probably honed through past life experiences. But though a seasoned Kung Fu practitioner might avoid locking eyes with such a person, they would never shy away from continually taking in the whole picture, watching that person's every movement in a subtle fashion. You never want to be blind to an unfolding scenario. Looking away during a potential encounter—especially out of fear—can cost you valuable time and real estate in your response, should your personal space be breeched before you can react. Kung Fu practitioners strive to never relinquish control of their circumstances or surroundings to an opponent. Instead, we deal with conflict on our own terms, trusting in our Kung Fu to put us in the optimal position, both to deal with and avoid such events.

We often choose to use our actual voices in self-defense situations. You might calmly speak to someone who is showing signs that they could become a threat. That's one way of exercising an aspect of control, with you dictating the tone. Or you might decide that a situation calls for a booming voice, maybe even one that uses some extremely harsh language, to dissuade someone. Obviously, your personality will have an influence upon your voice. But your instantaneous choices will largely be about your Kung Fu—what you are feeling, interpreting, and anticipating at the moment you decide that you need to engage.

NATURAL KUNG FU: LANGUAGE AND OUR BRAINS

In learning Kung Fu, you will start to pick up the names of varying techniques and concepts inherent to the art. Congratulations, you're on the road to acquiring basic words in Cantonese!

Bringing another language into your life can influence you in many positive ways. For example, people who speak more than one language often develop strong cognitive abilities, tend to have a more open-minded view of the world, and are well suited as multitaskers.

Now I'm not saying that learning Kung Fu will make you bilingual, because it certainly won't. But your brain will be working its mental muscles to acquire the terms and their proper pronunciation. So don't be the type of student who says, "I used the straight-out arm with my palm opened flat." Instead, call the technique by its correct name, *tan sau*.

Professor Ellen Bialystok, a distinguished researcher in the field of psychology at York University in Toronto, Canada, was kind enough to speak to us on the subject of acquiring language. "Every single experience you have as a human changes something about your mind and brain," said Professor Bialystok. "It's inevitable. So no one should be surprised that the languages we speak, and the way we use language, also changes our mind and brain. After all, using language is what we do with most of our waking hours.

"If you're bilingual, all the languages you are able to speak are simultaneously active in your brain. It creates a situation where we should be continually confused and picking the wrong languages. But we know that bilinguals don't make those mistakes," she continued. "That's because the system in your brain that's responsible for what you're paying attention to starts developing the minute you're born. *Who will feed me? Pick me up? Give me a hug?* From the beginning, the attention system of those infants being raised in an environment where multiple languages are spoken is different from those raised in an environment with just one language. We can measure and document those differences. So the bilingual experience can change the way your brain interprets things through your entire lifespan."

So what about the idea of picking up words and phrases in another language later in life through a particular study, such as learning Kung Fu?

"Well, it won't make you bilingual and it won't change your brain. But the secret to successful cognitive aging is to maintain a high level of cognitive ability. To remain active and engaged in things that keep your mind and brain healthy. In short, anything that's hard for your brain, is good for your brain," noted Professor Bialystok.

PAUL'S PERSPECTIVE: A MEASURED RESPONSE

As a high school English teacher, I've taught in many places where you have to set strict boundaries, including Rikers Island, New York City's largest jail, and several day drug rehab centers. Over the years, numerous teens have become angry with me because I refused to let them control any classroom or space in which I was in charge. I've been threatened a number of times, usually by someone brand new to the environment, someone under intense pressure, who hadn't had a chance to build a relationship with me yet.

Over time, I developed a rather even-tempered response to those spur-of-the-moment, volcano-like threats. With a solid posture, while making complete eye contact with the teen, I'd reply, "Try not to hurt me, I'm such a nice guy."

In actuality, those words were a semi-challenge back in their direction. It let everyone in the room know that I was going to stand my ground. Only it was so low-key that the angered teen on the receiving end could accept it, and perhaps convince themselves that they had triumphed in some small way. That type of response also left the door open for me to better connect with them later on, often during the same class period after they had a chance to calm down and reevaluate their surroundings. Because if you kick everyone out of your class who's ever had a bad moment, you'll soon be standing there alone, and therefore, totally useless.

LIFE APPLICATIONS

- You're a good singer. At karaoke night you get up to perform a song by one of your favorite pop stars. That's when you come to fully understand that your gift of song doesn't include the ability to hit the same high notes as your singing idol. On the walk back to your table, you decide that the next time you take the karaoke stage, you'll sing to your own strengths, and not someone else's.
- At a business meeting attended by lots of people, one of your coworkers raises their voice to you concerning an issue on which you have different opinions. Instead of raising your voice in return, you respond in a calm and even tone, adding a palpable pause for effect. This communicates to everyone that you are displeased, but not about to lower your standards concerning appropriateness.
- Someone stops you on the street and obviously needs help. That person speaks only Spanish, but you don't. You know a few Spanish words because you live in a community where a good number of Hispanics reside. The miscommunication is incredibly frustrating for both you and the person in need. So the next day, you decide to begin learning more Spanish.
- You're sitting at a crowded holiday dinner table with extended family. Someone brings up the fact that a couple

there will soon celebrate their fortieth wedding anniversary. The speaker goes on to say that they can't wait to celebrate with the couple. Only that celebration is already planned, coming in the form of a surprise party. You're not completely sure that the speaker knows that. So you look directly at him, making full eye contact, while tightly fixing your lips together. Reading your body language, the speaker stops for an instant and then changes the topic.

Our language is the reflection of ourselves. A language is an exact reflection of the character and growth of its speakers.
—Cesar Chavez, labor leader and activist

A MOSTLY ORAL TRADITION
For centuries, the history of Chinese martial arts—its systems, styles, techniques, and lineage—was passed down, almost exclusively, via the spoken word. This includes generations upon generations of Shaolin monks, who produced no recorded manuals and, instead, passed down knowledge directly from the voice and example of teaching masters to the ears and eyes of practicing students.

The earliest written documentation of Wing Chun Kung Fu doesn't arrive until the nineteenth century. In fact, a highly prized axiom of the art praises this passionate human chain responsible for securing its roots in future fertile ground. That axiom is *Wing Chun Chuen Jing Tung*, and translates as "Wing Chun authentically passing down."

The legendary Ip Man saw the world of martial arts changing and began to invest time and effort in supplementing theoral tradition. Prior to his passing in 1972, Ip

(continued next page)

Man had students film him demonstrating several Wing Chun forms. Ip Man also commissioned his student, Moy Yat, to carve many of the art's maxims, referred to as *kuen kuit*, onto chops or seals, which could be used to print when inked. In the original Cantonese, these maxims resemble a short, single-verse song/poem that rhymes, so it can be easily remembered and propagated among students.

Below is an example of those maxims, chosen by their reflection of material and ideas already presented in this text. We'll examine others in forthcoming chapters.

A strong attitude and posture gives an advantage over your opponent.

Have confidence and your calmness will dominate the situation.

If you don't train hard when you're young, you will have nothing when you're old.

HONORED GUEST: SAMMO HUNG (HONG KONG)

If, up until now, your understanding of Kung Fu has come from the world of entertainment, then you've most likely been influenced by famed actor, director, choreographer, and martial artist Sammo Hung (Hung Kam-bo), a living legend in the Chinese film industry. At the age of nine, Hung joined the Peking Opera School, becoming the lead member of their adolescent performance group, where he would begin a lifelong friendship with an even younger member who would eventually assume the stage name Jackie Chan (Chan Kong-sang).

"My upbringing in the Peking Opera School gave me a great foundation of acrobatic skills

(continued next page)

Live Life Like a Kung Fu Master

and agility," said Hung. "I'm not a Kung Fu master who studied a particular form of martial arts. I'm a filmmaker with a very diverse martial arts background. I started out as a stuntman while I was still in school, and I fell in love with moviemaking."

Early in his career, however, Hung became aware of his own limitations as it pertained to his knowledge of the arts, and began to immerse himself in study.

"I realized that the Kung Fu I knew was insufficient to support the creativity I wanted to express on the screen, so I started spending more time and effort studying different forms of Kung Fu, enhancing my knowledge. Learning these different schools and disciplines of martial arts helped me greatly in choreographing my action movies."

What was Hung's main goal in his presentation of Kung Fu to a broad audience?

"I wanted my audience to leave the cinema feeling happy. Hopefully, they would find many of the fight scenes exciting, enjoying the storylines and relating to the characters I helped create. When my movies entertain people, I feel happy too."

In fact, Hung takes a lot of pride in being able to present Chinese martial arts, which he considers to have great value, to people worldwide.

"Like many different sports, I believe that martial arts is good for all youngsters to learn. It's a form of exercise which strengthens both the mind and the body. It also helps to develop essential qualities in people such as self-confidence, self-awareness, and endurance," said Hung. "And obviously, it's not just about fighting. Every style has a theory and philosophy behind its teaching. It's not meant to be a weapon, but rather a discipline."

Now in his seventies, Sammo Hung has been part of approximately 130 films, including portraying Master

(continued next page)

The Language of Kung Fu

Hung Chun-Nam in *Ip Man 2* (2010). And though he firmly believes that martial arts is intended for everyone, he is quick to point out that each individual's journey will be different.

"Depending on your effort and the form of martial arts you're learning, there will be different insights and benefits from your exposure to Kung Fu," noted Hung. "It all comes down to the individual, not the culture."

CHAPTER THREE

THE LITTLE BEGINNING IDEA
(*SIU NIM TAO*)

An idea that is developed and put into action is more important than an idea that exists only as an idea.

—Buddha

ALL JOURNEYS BEGIN SOMEWHERE. Understanding the alphabet undoubtedly came after you could communicate using words. And that's exactly how it will be with your introduction to *Siu Nim Tao*, the figurative alphabet of Wing Chun. This form will be your touchstone for bringing the simplicity of Kung Fu into all of your daily activities. Many practitioners of the art perform it every day, continually grounding and focusing themselves through all it has to offer.

PHYSICAL ATTRIBUTES

Siu Nim Tao, often referred to as "The Little Beginning Idea," is more than just the opening form of Wing Chun Kung Fu. In a sense, it also serves as the art's alphabet, introducing both the body and mind to the foundational techniques, structures, and movements that can be viewed as its letters. Over time, with practice and experience, my goal for you is to use your growing familiarity with these letters to soon build words in the form of Kung Fu responses. As your skill and knowledge increases, you will use these same letters/movements to eventually build whole sentences through your coordinated physical responses.

Though *Siu Nim Tao* is the focus of this individual chapter, in reality, several books could be written on this topic alone. So I'll stick to its basics, such as how the form can better your Kung Fu and your daily life, fully understanding that my words will be supplemented by the YouTube video of me performing *Siu Nim Tao*. For students just starting out upon their Kung Fu journey, actually seeing it done correctly, along with a commentary to accompany the visual, will ease the process of translating the descriptions herein to physical movements.

> *For a visual demonstration, go to YouTube and search: "Live Life Like a Kung Fu Master—William Moy, Siu Nim Tao."*

The form opens with the practitioner assuming a stance called *yee jee kim yeung ma*. With the fists (palm sides up) held horizontally and chambered, almost beneath your arm pits, bring your feet and knees together. Then sink your body weight, thus lowering your center of gravity. Using your heels, turn the toes outward approximately forty-five degrees. Next, turn the heels outward approximately forty-five degrees, using your toes as pivot points. In doing so, you've created a triangle between your feet from the knees to your lower legs. In Cantonese, *yee* means two, and the alphabetical character for it is a shorter line running parallel above a slightly longer line, mirroring the pair of triangles you've just formed.

The Little Beginning Idea (Siu Nim Tao)

Tuck your pelvis beneath your spine and grip the floor with your feet, while squeezing your knees together and keeping the spine straight, as if you were riding a horse—the literal meaning of *ma*. The *yeung* means "goat," because for generations this is how Chinese farmers, who lived on floating barges, corralled their livestock (goats and sheep) for shearing and other tasks by clamping *(kim)* them between their knees and lower legs.

The result of performing the stance correctly will figuratively turn your body into a bow string that has been drawn back with an arrow ready to be released. There's forward tension in your lower body, which if not for your pelvis holding you back, would spring forward. As a novice, until you develop a strong horse, you may even feel tremors in your legs from the strain. Meanwhile, your upper body—like the hand of the archer—is relatively relaxed.

It's important to stress that the *yee jee kim yeung ma* stance is used solely used for training purposes, never for fighting. Why? Though it builds stability in the practitioner, it affords little to no mobility.

Siu Nim Tao is partly comprised of several techniques we've discussed in the prior two chapters—the straight punch (*yat je jung choi*), *tan sau*, and *fuk sau*—which are performed first on the left side of the body and then the right, training each side equally. The form also introduces us to *huen sau*, a technique in which the hand circles from the wrist, clearing the center line and allowing the practitioner to change position while maintaining control of the opponent's arm.

These movements are normally done very slowly, almost like a meditation. It could last anywhere from a few minutes to twenty minutes or beyond. Why do it slowly? Because it helps build our internal energy and mental focus.

Beginner's often ask, "Sifu, what should I be concentrating on during this meditative-like sequence?" The answer? "Center line. Center line. Center line."

In fact, moving your *tan sau* into position, from where the fist was originally chambered near the armpit, will help you find and develop a natural arm slot in the middle of your body. From there, the elbow will follow behind the wrist as you claim the center line. The more you practice, the more you'll stretch and strengthen those muscles and tendons to better fully occupy that valuable space.

The form goes on to introduce a host of new techniques, as well as the previously encountered *bong sau* (arched wing hand). The middle to latter portions of *Siu Nim Tao* are performed at a faster speed, but still in a relaxed fashion without a pointed emphasis on power. Its primary goal is to create muscle memory until the movements flow almost instinctually and without thought. It also teaches the practitioner to regain the center line from both a weak and dominant position.

Overall, *Siu Nim Tao* builds internal power, strengthens our legs, improves posture, teaches us economy of motion, relieves

The Little Beginning Idea (Siu Nim Tao)

stress, and opens the door for us to perform Kung Fu with a clear mind. The form is also the start of recognizing a different feeling in each of your hands, something that will boost your ability to defend yourself, and can become a teaching model for multitasking in your everyday endeavors.

FROM MY LIFE: LEARNING TO TAKE MY TIME

I first learned *Siu Nim Tao* as an adolescent. My father taught it to me over the course of many months, in stages, giving me additional sequences only when I was absolutely ready to move forward. Unfortunately, at the time, I didn't have the patience to appreciate what he was doing for my Kung Fu: building an immensely strong foundation. One day, I asked my father if we could speed up the process, and he answered me with a rather stern rejection.

My young mind and short attention span found the form's movements of *tan sau* and *fuk sau* to be boring, with the elongated time spent on playing these slow, relaxed techniques less than exciting. But I stuck with it, just as I had been instructed, playing the complete form thousands of times over the years.

By the time I got to college, my perspective on the form had totally evolved. Whenever I felt the pressure of academic classes (projects, papers, finals), my part-time job, or social responsibilities, I'd take time out to play *Siu Nim Tao* for a half hour or so. I discovered that it not only cleared my mind, it blocked out negative external forces and helped me to refocus. It didn't eliminate these challenges in my life. Instead, it helped me to keep them in perspective.

Today, I've found that a lifetime of playing the form has enabled me to activate a relaxation response, both physically and mentally, bringing about a state of calmness through just a few of its simple movements.

No matter what the world throws in my path, I always have *Siu Nim Tao* in my back pocket. Wonderfully, it is something

Live Life Like a Kung Fu Master

that has become stronger and more vital with my experience and growing age.

Whenever I have a distinguished Kung Fu visitor to my school, I usually request the honor of seeing their *Siu Nim Tao*. I find that it's like a window into someone's Kung Fu to see their personal expression of the form and how it becomes a part of them. In return, either I or one of my senior students will play it as well, in an exchange of respect.

My fondest wish is that you discover a similar value in this form, develop a desire to play it every day, and come to fully understand how much this "little beginning idea" can offer the practitioner.

> *My ideas usually come not at my desk writing but in the midst of living.*
>
> —Anais Nin, French essayist and novelist

10,000 HOURS TO SECOND NATURE

Whenever we tackle the task of learning a new skill—be it for our jobs or personal enjoyment—we normally start by acquainting ourselves with the fundamentals, breaking the activity down piece by piece, often to its most basic elements. From there, we improve our abilities through repetition.

You're probably familiar with author and journalist Malcolm Gladwell's book *Outliers* and his "10,000-hour rule." It states that achieving true expertise in almost anything is a matter of practicing for ten thousand hours. That's very much in line with the literal definition of Kung Fu: *time and effort equals a skill*. Whether it's a new computer program with a slightly different menu, learning to be a short-order cook with a line of hungry customers during the dinner rush, or understanding how to stay out of the kitchen on a pickleball court, our bodies and brains need time to immerse themselves and adjust.

The Little Beginning Idea (Siu Nim Tao)

With enough time and practice, our actions and reactions can become almost instinctual.

Consider the daily activities that some of us accomplish with little to no mental or physical preparation. Maybe you can expertly tie a necktie in seconds without glancing at a mirror. Perhaps you can slide your hand up and down the neck of a guitar to the proper fret, changing finger positions to play each chord correctly while singing at the same time. That's amazing. Now, take someone who's never done either of those activities before and watch them struggle.

How would you teach them to succeed?

How would you teach yourself to do something at which you possessed almost no experience?

Well, first you'd most likely learn the correct techniques involved, followed by hours of practice. Of course, practicing correctly will shorten the learning curve. That's where a teacher, coach, or sifu might come in handy.

Kung Fu practitioners have a saying to describe impatient beginners: *Everybody wants their Kung Fu yesterday.*

Unfortunately, that's just not possible. Even intellectual prodigies don't completely master the alphabet on their first day of kindergarten. But understanding that mountains can be climbed over the course of time, no matter how high they might appear today, is one of the greatest lessons for people who passionately want something more in their lives.

NATURAL KUNG FU: SEVEN LETTERS AT A TIME

Many people are familiar with using the alphabet to play word games such as Scrabble, Boggle, and Wordle. Like *Siu Nim Tao's* relationship to building a Kung Fu response, understanding how certain combinations of letters fit together can both improve your language skills and help you to succeed at these alphabet-based games.

Live Life Like a Kung Fu Master

Joel Wapnick is a World Scrabble Champion who polishes his abilities through daily study and practice.

"I like to memorize words. Right now, I have a list of sixteen thousand words that I've memorized in sequence, and I'd like to increase that to twenty-four thousand words. I rehearse the list on long walks. I also like to study anagrams, approximately three hundred words a day," said Wapnick, whose high score at Scrabble is an astounding 715 points.

Consistency and a solid sense of board vision have helped Wapnick to hone his in-game skills to a superior level.

"I arrange my tiles with the vowels on the left and consonants on the right. That gives me consistency because when I study words, I study them in that form as well. So it makes it easier for me to recognize what I might have in my rack, or in combination with the board," noted Wapnick, who averages three *Bingos* per game, Scrabble slang for when a player uses all seven tiles in his rack to earn a fifty-point bonus. "Having board vision is really important. That means knowing how to place tiles in between two rows, seeing an opening on the board, and knowing when to close one. It's crucial in becoming a strong player."

Cesar Del Solar is also an elite Scrabble player, having quickly won several tournaments in his young career. He grew up speaking Spanish as part of a family that immigrated to the US from Venezuela. Cesar's father believed that education would be the key to his children's future success, so academic pursuits were strongly encouraged. As a result, Del Solar received a scholarship to CalTech to study engineering. That's where he began to play Scrabble online as an escape from the stress of his collegiate classes.

Cesar, who grew up participating in martial arts, relates the game of Scrabble to real-life activities.

"Sometimes you make a bad play, especially in a tournament when you're competing under the clock. You have to be able to put that play aside and refocus, go back to your basic strengths.

[34]

There's a definite psychology to it," said Del Solar, who arranges his tiles alphabetically in his rack, the same way he studies lists of words and flash cards.

If you ever challenge an elite player to a game of Scrabble, be prepared. Always playing to the best of their abilities contributes to their overall consistency.

"I never take it easy on anyone, though I rarely play amateurs or less than serious players," noted Wapnick, who in a recent game played a ten-letter word, *retirement*, by adding r-e-t-i-r-n-t to the eme (a noun meaning an uncle or friend) already on the board. "Scrabble is a word game. But it's also a math and spatial game as well. The words are rules and there's more than 100,000 rules."

PAUL'S PERSPECTIVE: NO IDEA

I was doing *Siu Nim Tao* on the beach one morning, executing the form just a foot or so into the waterline when I had an interesting experience. Because of the constant in-and-out motion of the tide, there are forces being exerted upon your balance, sometimes in simultaneous directions. In addition, the sand beneath your bare feet is constantly shifting with the tide's push and pull, realigning the sandy bottom's ever-changing face.

I was probably midway through the form when an older gentleman who was walking along the shore with his dog said to me, in a matter-of-fact tone as he passed, "That kind of fighting is no good. There's no force in those punches. Everything you're doing is too soft. You'll never defend yourself like that."

The man didn't wait for any type of answer from me, and never broke his stride. He just kept walking on his way, with his dog following alongside.

Siu Nim Tao is called the "Little Beginning Idea," and I would have been happy to share with him my thoughts on why I believed the form was a good investment of my time and energy.

But on that day, this gentleman wasn't interested in an *idea*, or a new way of possibly looking at things. He was simply interested in a one-way communication, one in which he knew everything and had all the right answers. So I did not call after him to start a conversation. Instead, I simply let the unenlightened moment pass.

After finishing the form that morning and, in a self-evaluation of my performance, I felt there were some things I could have done better. But, overall, I felt satisfied, having adjusted for both the ocean's many forces and the little bit of ill-informed wind stirred up by that passerby.

LIFE APPLICATIONS

- You're baffled as to the meaning of a particular word in an article you're reading. So you break the word down into its simplest terms, examining its prefix, root, and suffix in an effort to piece together a possible definition.
- You understand that a neighbor living down the block from you is deaf. You've nodded hello and goodbye to them several times recently. In an effort to improve communications and better yourself, you start to view online videos about signing, and print out a chart detailing the American Sign Language alphabet.
- After straining your shoulder, the doctor gives you a prescription for physical therapy where the PT assigns you several basic exercises to do, a few times each week, using just a two-pound weight in order to slowly build up strength in the area.
- Your inner resolve to reach certain goals has begun to waver recently. In response, you set aside twenty minutes per day to clear your mind and meditate on what it is that

The Little Beginning Idea (Siu Nim Tao)

you really want to achieve, and how much you're actually willing to sacrifice to attain those goals.

If you have an apple and I have an apple and we exchange these apples then you and I will still each have one apple. But if you have an idea and I have an idea and we exchange these ideas, then each of us will have two ideas.
  —George Bernard Shaw, Irish playwright and poet

A PAIR OF LEGENDARY WOMEN

During the early eighteenth century, there lived a Buddhist nun named Ng Mui who was forced to flee the Shaolin Temple when it was destroyed during the Qing Dynasty by government officials (believing the sanctuary harbored revolutionaries). Ng Mui was regarded as one of China's top martial artists at the time. Legend has it that this observant and forward-thinking woman believed it was possible to devise a system of fighting that wasn't reliant on a practitioner possessing brute strength—a type of thought most likely to be conceived by a woman.

Borrowing her example from the natural world, it is said that Ng Mui became inspired to devise such an art after she witnessed a fight between a stork and small rodent (often the legend replaces the rodent with a snake). It was a skirmish in which Ng Mui observed the water fowl using its ample wings for the purposes of both offense and defense, something she would consciously incorporate into her system.

The art was taught to a woman named Yim Wing Chun, who was being pressured by a warlord to become his bride. The legend says that Yim Wing Chun used the fledgling system to defeat the powerful

(continued next page)

Live Life Like a Kung Fu Master

warlord in hand-to-hand combat, freeing herself from his unwanted proposal.

Whenever something as meaningful as a new martial art is devised—especially in a culturewhere passing along knowledge is primarily dependent on an oral tradition—one of the main concerns is how such a system can survive past the lifespan of its originator. That answer flowered in the form of training students who could one day propagate the art in future fields.

Yim Wing Chun was that precious seedling for Ng Mui. Hence, the art of Wing Chun, which is purported to be the only martial art invented by a woman, bears her name.

CHAPTER FOUR

WHY A KUNG FU FAMILY?

Family is not an important thing. It's everything.
—Michael J. Fox, actor and advocate

A S A SIFU, I relish the role of teaching you right from wrong in this art, and giving you a solid foundation to address the many challenges in learning Kung Fu. Hopefully you'll transfer that knowledge to your daily tasks and interactions with others, creating an extended network of friends and acquaintances wherever you go.

PHYSICAL ATTRIBUTES

I normally begin class by working on a skill or technique that everyone in attendance can experience. Then we break up into pairs to practice what I've just introduced. That's the start of building a family relationship. Within that pairing, one of the participants will undoubtedly have more experience than the other. Like an older brother or sister at home might clarify how to perform

Live Life Like a Kung Fu Master

a simple household chore to a younger sibling, the more experienced practitioner will lead their partner, fixing potential mistakes and offering feedback.

In Kung Fu culture, your elders have specific titles. Your older Kung Fu brother can be addressed as *si hing* (pronounced *cee-hing*), and your older sister as *si jai* (*cee-jay*). What makes them older? It has nothing to do with age. Rather, the order is established by who entered the door first and joined the school/family. On your very first day in class, you will be everyone's *si dai* (*cee-die*), their young brother or sister. If another student comes to class for the first time several days later, you will automatically become their older sibling. They will be your *si dai*.

The overwhelming majority of time that you're training in class, you'll be running techniques, doing exercises, and putting your hands into the hands of your classmates, not the sifu, who will be carefully observing the process. Your older siblings will be passing down the knowledge they've gained to you, with a type of *pay it forward* mentality. Why would they have such an interest in *your* Kung Fu? For one, they know what it's like to struggle with the complexities of learning the art. And by bringing you along to a higher level, they'll hopefully soon have another worthy and challenging partner with whom to train and test their skills. That's how respectful and flourishing relationships between students of all abilities allows great Kung Fu to cultivate and be transmitted.

FROM MY LIFE: WIDENING A STUDENT'S RELATIONSHIPS

For most of my career as a sifu, I've been fortunate enough to operate a pair of Kung Fu schools, one in the Chinatown section of Manhattan and one in the Bayside section of Queens, another of the five boroughs that comprise New York City. Those classes

Why a Kung Fu Family?

would normally be attended by anywhere from fifteen to twenty-five students. But I've also taught many students privately. That's because many students either have very demanding schedules and can only meet at certain times, or possess a natural inclination to shy away from learning in large groups.

Deandre was a private student of mine who immediately took to Kung Fu, seeing it have a positive influence in both his personal and professional life. But after many months of hard work, I noticed him beginning to plateau in his Kung Fu and his excitement in learning, most likely believing he'd reached his destination. So I brought together a trio of my private students so they could experience training with partners other than myself.

The three of them seemed to enjoy the experience, but Deandre was considerably more talented than the other two students and could control them rather easily. And again, after a few weeks, he was wondering if his learning was complete. That's when I encouraged Deandre to experience a week or two as part of my regular classes and see the progress of many different students. Because, despite all of his dedicated training, he had missed out on the benefits of being part of a functioning Kung Fu family. He had no *si hings* or *si jais* to help guide and push him to be even better. The pair of students with whom he trained as part of the "trio" were technically Deandre's *si dai*. But he hadn't felt the bond of helping them learn from the beginning, because they'd also been training privately.

Deandre hesitantly accepted my offer. That first night of class was packed, and he touched hands with more people over a two-hour period than he had in all of his training time combined. I watched him closely. He had moments of both exhilaration (when he controlled others) and frustration (when others controlled him), especially a female student who was half his size. He also encountered several students who were just above or below his level, and I could sense him gravitating toward them.

[41]

Live Life Like a Kung Fu Master

A new student enrolled that evening, and I assigned Deandre to teach her our opening exercise, the *pak* drill (I'll explain this drill later on in the text). This way he could have some sweat equity in bringing that student along—in a sense his first *si dai*. In turn, one of Deandre's new *si hings* took an interest in him, offering to help Deandre with his footwork and horse.

Without looking back, Deandre quickly changed his training regime from private lessons to attending class with others. He'd probably come to that first class feeling a bit like an only child, but I believe that he left embracing the dutiful giving and rewards of being part of a Kung Fu family.

> *Family isn't always blood. It's the people in your life who want you in theirs.*
> —Maya Angelou, writer, poet, and civil rights activist

BUSINESS AND SPORTING TIES

The workplace can often mirror a family dynamic. You've probably heard someone refer to a coworker as their "work wife, "work husband," or "work mom," emphasizing the closeness of their relationship during business hours. Remember, people are always happier in an atmosphere of trust and caring, where the common goal is for everyone to succeed and move forward. That's productivity at its best.

For many people, their first real job is at a fast-food restaurant. Establishments like Burger King, Taco Bell, Subway, Domino's, Wendy's, and Dunkin' are responsible for giving generations of teens their first jobs. In addition to the training of teens, McDonald's is famous for its "Hamburger University," an eight-campus training facility for franchise owners and their managers. Their shared training results in consistency of product and organization.

[42]

Why a Kung Fu Family?

One credo of the school is that people remember best what they learn first. Hence, learning to do something the wrong way will result in a longer period of time in relearning to do it correctly (some studies claim it's five times longer). That includes an exacting eye for detail in assembling the Big Mac. What's the right order? Spread the secret sauce on the bottom base. Then top with chopped onion, shredded lettuce, slice of cheese, beef patty, and some pickle slices. Top the second bun with more sauce, onion, lettuce, pickles, and beef patty before finishing with sauce and the third bun. That's right, only one slice of cheese is used on the Big Mac.

Hungry for more?

Consider the brother and sister Basketball Hall of Fame duo of Reggie and Cheryl Miller. As youngsters, the incredibly talented pairing used to play two-on-two against unsuspecting adult competitors at their local park in Riverside, California, for ten dollars a game, ultimately using their winnings to buy Happy Meals at Mickey D's after a long Saturday on the courts.

Cheryl, who is one year Reggie's senior, learned to play basketball at the feet of her two older brothers. Neither of them cut Cheryl any slack, blocking her shots unmercifully until their five-year-old sister ran off crying. In turn, Cheryl showed Reggie the same type of tough love to which she'd been introduced when it came to competing on the court, often drubbing her younger brother by large winning margins in games of one-on-one in front of his friends.

During his Hall of Fame induction speech, an appreciative Reggie Miller said, "I lived across the hall from absolutely, positively, the greatest woman basketball player ever. I'm proud to say I am not on this stage if it wasn't for you, Cheryl Deann [Miller]."

And don't forget about the NFL teams with rookie or young quarterbacks still learning their craft. Many franchises in this position sign veteran backup or even third-string quarterbacks at

[43]

Live Life Like a Kung Fu Master

the end of their careers. Why? Their years of experience can be incredibly useful in the mentoring process of their younger teammates at the same position. Several such older QBs have made massive contributions to their team's fortunes without ever setting foot on the field themselves during an actual game.

NATURAL KUNG FU: DO NO HARM

Dr. Alberto Cayton, recipient of the 2000 Walter E. Reed Medal for Excellence in Medicine, immigrated to the US from the Philippines in 1968, and began practicing surgery on these shores in 1975. Martial arts are important and well respected in Dr. Cayton's country of origin, so he made sure that his three children participated as part of their youth.

"It's very important to study a martial art. It gives you confidence in yourself and your abilities," said Dr. Cayton. "It's a building block for your future."

As a surgeon on the staff of Brooklyn Hospital, where he also taught medical students, Dr. Cayton had more than five hundred residents train beneath him. How does the average residency program for young doctors mirror being part of a Kung Fu family? It's all about the sharing of knowledge and how it gets passed down.

"Residents learn a lot from the established doctors with whom they work and train. Being a resident, which can last anywhere from three to five years, is like an apprenticeship. You're continuing to learn in your specialty area, whether that's surgery, pediatrics, internal medicine or something else," said Dr. Cayton. "Medicine is a dynamic field. It's so vast, and always changing in one way or another with new techniques constantly being developed."

It's an intense and sustained learning process. Residents sometimes work twenty-hour shifts in the hospital, with occasional workweeks totaling as much as eighty hours. That means for stretches at a time, most of their waking hours are spent on the hospital floor, learning, responding and becoming immersed in the practice of medicine.

"The field of medical professionals is like a large family. There is a lot of sharing of information and experiences, all with the same purpose—to help the patient be healthier," noted Dr. Cayton, who dedicated his life and surgical abilities to his patients and students for nearly half a century.

Sadly, Dr. Alberto Cayton passed away in July 2024. But in that larger family spirit by which he lived his life, Dr. Cayton's final act was to donate his liver to a stranger in need.

PAUL'S PERSPECTIVE: FIRST FAMILY IMPRESSIONS

As an ardent basketball player, I learned how to use my hips to create leverage and take away space from much bigger opponents. I clearly wasn't stronger or more athletic than my competition, but I had perfected that particular skill over many hours of serious play. One day, I glanced over to the sideline to see two people engaged in what turned out to be Kung Fu exercises. I was taken by the fact that they appeared to be using positioning over raw strength. One of that pair noticed my keen interest and later on offered to teach me some basic Kung Fu. We had probably met four or five times to practice, and I was really enjoying myself. Then I received the news that my teacher had torn his ACL playing basketball, and our lessons would need to take a hiatus, most likely for a full year.

In serendipitous fashion, those circumstances led me to the door of Sifu William's school. I liked William right away, and discovered that we both shared a passion for writing. William explained to me, though, that the Kung Fu I had been learning was from a slightly different lineage, and that I would need to make some minor adjustments in technique.

Live Life Like a Kung Fu Master

Later that day, near the end of my first class, one of the senior students with whom I'd been training, my new *si hing*, asked me if I had ever studied Kung Fu before, because he thought I did the opening exercise better than the average beginner. I must have used a term from the other lineage in my reply. Seemingly distressed by this, I later heard him warn another student that I could be a spy participating for just a few classes to see how things are done here. I thought that notion was absolutely silly. Only his seemingly far-fetched conjecture came with some immediate consequences, as I noticed several of the other students shy away from working with me.

Three days later, I showed up for my next class forty-five minutes early, with a specific plan in mind to assuage the trepidations of my classmates. Several of the more experienced students were already there, training with each other. One of them politely told me that class hadn't officially started yet, and I should come back at the appointed time. "I didn't come early to train," I answered. "I came early to be respectful and clean the school." That's when I took a bottle of glass cleaner from my gym bag and began to wipe down the large-mirrored wall. After that, I cleaned all of the windows and then swept the entire floor.

When class officially began, I understood that the fruits of my labors had quickly blossomed. There was a line of several experienced students waiting to work with me, and one soon offered to stay after class to give me extra time.

Did I feel bad about that slight manipulation of the people who would become my Kung Fu family? Maybe. But that's the way it can be in families, especially when your brothers and sisters don't have a perfectly clear vision of you yet. Words may not be enough to set the situation straight. Instead, you might need to clarify the lines of communication through your deeds and actions, even if those actions are by design.

[46]

Why a Kung Fu Family?

LIFE APPLICATIONS

- At your job, you're put in charge of a brand-new intern who'll be helping to lighten the load in your department. By investing the time and effort to train that intern properly, you'll be helping your department, your company, and yourself by means of increasing productivity, and by potentially not having to redo the work of a poorly trained newbie.
- Because of scheduling, you're forced to take a class with a college professor who has a reputation for giving students a grade no higher than a B. So you turn to one of your sorority sisters who had that same professor two semesters ago, asking for an assessment on the class, her past notes, and the types of papers and exams that were assigned.
- Part of the joy of visiting your grandparents is the amazing comfort food they always serve. On this visit, however, instead of those savory dishes being in the refrigerator ready to eat, their individual ingredients are on the kitchen counter, along with an apron. You're about to get a lesson on how to prepare those fabulous dishes, so that you can pass them on to future generations of your family.
- You come across a flyer that reads: Apply to become a plumber's or electrician's apprentice. Learn from a master of these arts to secure a profitable and challenging career.

This is my family. I found it all on my own.

—Stitch, Disney film *Lilo & Stitch*

Live Life Like a Kung Fu Master

IF THE SHOE FITS

The Kung Fu tradition of respecting one's elders (*sifu, si hing, si jai*) undoubtedly finds its roots in the Confucian ethic of Filial piety, which states that children should care for their parents and elders, respecting and working hard in their name, just as their parents and elders did for them when they were too young to care for themselves.

As a reflection of this, I remember meeting my father and several of his students for a late afternoon lunch, after a long morning training session. My father was sitting in the restaurant showing everyone a new pair of sneakers that he was wearing. He proudly proclaimed that they were given to him by a generous student. We all agreed with my father that it was a wonderful gesture, but as my father continued to glow about the gift, the rest of us looked at one another, realizing that this particular student owned a sporting goods store, and that giving his sifu a simple pair of sneakers probably didn't deserve this level of adulation.

But as my father continued on with his praise, it became clear to the rest of us why he was so moved. "My student told me that this is the exact same style and brand of sneaker that he gave to his own father as a gift."

Thus, the act implied that this student held his sifu, his Kung Fu parent, in a similar regard to his own father. What higher praise could my father, Moy Yat, who modeled his Kung Fu family after the nuclear family, hope to receive?

HONORED GUEST: KAREN SHEPERD (LOS ANGELES COUNTY, CALIFORNIA)

Professor Karen Sheperd, an eighth-degree Black Belt in the art of Wun Hop Kuen Do Kung Fu (a blend of Chinese, Japanese, and Filipino influences), has not only stamped herself as one of the great martial artists of our time, but was also the driving force behind establishing competitive ratings for women. That wholly increased the number of female participants at martial arts tournaments, giving them tangible goals for which to strive.

The journey began for Karen when she needed a few elective credits in high school. "I was somehow pointed towards martial arts during a time when women didn't really do them. I had to choose a class for credits, and there was a listing for Shotokan Karate. I didn't know anything about martial arts at that point, but I was really excited about it."

How did the fledgling student, and future world champion, do in her first class?

"The moves came so naturally to me. The instructor said I had natural ability and that I should continue to study. But my father was against it, because that's not what girls did back then, and I couldn't afford to continue on my own."

Just a few years later, while attending the University of Oregon, Karen joined a school club team doing Kajukenbo, a striking art that incorporates grappling and joint locks. She also found an instructor on campus teaching Tai Chi, and in her free time immersed herself in both arts.

"We studied applications and real-world fighting. The movements really opened my mind. I was doing animal forms, alternating between a hard and soft style. Finding those training partners was more or less a miracle. It gave me a strong foundation, and it's what eventually made me a champion."

(continued next page)

Live Life Like a Kung Fu Master

Karen would make a name in the martial arts world by mastering forms, referred to as "Kata" in Japanese.

"Many traditional martial artists look down on forms. They say, 'That looks cute but what's the point?' They respect fighting more. But forms are really just a way of imagining that you're surrounded by opponents, and fighting. That's why in most forms you change directions," emphasized Karen. "The word *forms* is actually defined as a structured element, as in a work of art—to a standard of excellence based on experience. Forms are necessary to develop technique, and intense focus. For me, forms are the 'art' in martial arts."

When Karen started in forms competitions, she was the only woman rated in the national "Top 10." At the time, only 10 percent or so of competitive martial artists were women. She firmly believed there needed to be separate ratings for women and women's divisions to attract more females to the sport. So she took it upon herself to approach the sport's top-ranking bodies and sponsors. After successfully jumping every hurdle they placed in her way, Karen's aspiration of separate forms, weapons divisions, and national ratings for women became a reality.

Karen won numerous world championships, being rated No. 1 in Women's Black Belt Forms during 1979 and 1980. A year later, she was offered a co-starring role in the Japanese martial arts film *The Shinobi Ninja*, essentially becoming one of the very first female action stars.

"I was thrilled to do it, to go to Japan and be in a movie. The budget wasn't big and there were no stand-ins for the actors. I remember laying there in the snow on a Japanese mountain top with a fake arrow in my arm, thinking to myself, *This is amazing.* When I got back to the states, I moved to LA to study acting."

(continued next page)

Why a Kung Fu Family?

Karen was in a succession of films and TV shows, including being part of the cast of *Cyborg 2* (1993) with Angelina Jolie, whom Karen helped to prepare by teaching Angelina how to make a fist, throw a punch, and perform basic film fighting. Jolie went on to take the torch for female action stars into the new millennium.

But perhaps Karen's most memorable on-screen moment came in a dazzling fight sequence against the next female forms champion, Cynthia Rothrock, in the 1986 film *Above the Law*, shot in Hong Kong. The pair did battle some twenty-five feet in the air while balancing upon a freestanding scaffold.

"We were really up that high. It was full contact and intense. The director also gave us no opportunity to rehearse the scene. He just kept screaming, "Harder! Harder! Faster! Faster!' as we filmed. There were bruises, contusions, and injuries. We did have stunt doubles for the higher falls but, interestingly, they were all men. You can actually tell if you look closely."

How does her vast training in the martial arts aid Karen in daily life?

"I trained old-school style, pushing myself to the limits. I feel blessed that I had teachers who instilled a toughness in me. All of that continues with me today as I push through the obstacles of daily life. One of the schools that I attended has a clover leaf as its symbol. The three leaves represent body, mind, and spirit. I think of that combination today as I rely on my training and faith to approach everyday activities."

Karen has also added another element to her acting career by appearing in live theater. Naturally, there wasn't much opportunity for her to kick butt in the Tennessee Williams play, *Summer and Smoke*. So she needed to focus on other skills.

(continued next page)

Live Life Like a Kung Fu Master

"Being on stage like that was challenging and fun. In a sense, it was just like competing in martial arts, a real adrenaline rush. But I really had to do my homework, to know the lines and to pull out the little hidden secrets of my character. My training in the arts absolutely helped me to take on the challenge of live theater, because whatever happens, you have to keep going. And that's what makes a good martial artist."

CHAPTER FIVE

STRUCTURE AND POSITION

The higher your structure is to be, the deeper must be its foundation.

—Saint Augustine

POSITIVE RESULTS IN YOUR life are not accidental. They're normally achieved through dedication and hard work, which owe much of their stalwart reputation to doing things the right way, not haphazardly.

PHYSICAL ATTRIBUTES

Most people have seen more Kung Fu movies than they've seen real Kung Fu. The movies like to make Kung Fu, along with a host of other martial arts, appear somewhat mystical. In the movie industry's defense, I suppose that kind of otherworldly association makes for a better storyline, one that cashes in at the box office, filling more seats in theaters. *Real* Kung Fu is stunningly beautiful. I'm not speaking about overly elaborate movements, high spinning kicks, and that stereotypical vocalization of the practitioner at the moment of execution—*Hi-yah!* Compared to that media representation of the art, actual Kung Fu looks plain and ordinary to the untrained eye. Its true beauty lies in its effectiveness, especially waging combat in close quarters, a space where it's difficult for movie cameras to film action sequences and get good perspective.

So then, if it's not mystical, what is it that gives Kung Fu its power? The primary answer is found in the art's foundation of proper structure and position. This gives the practitioner the advantage of using their skeletal system, when properly aligned, to generate both power and incredible resistance to force. It also allows us to make greater use of our muscles and tendons, creating substantial chains of flexible strength that are constantly shifting shape, yet maintaining superior structure and position as we flow from one technique to another. For example, remember how the wrist remains perfectly and economically stationary, serving almost as a pivot point as we shift between the trio of core techniques: *tan sau, fuk sau* and *bong sau.*

One of the main tests of proper structure for both the *tan sau* and *fuk sau* is that your elbow, which should theoretically be on the center line, needs to be positioned a fist and a half away (approximately four to five inches) from your body. If the elbow position is too close, both techniques will collapse under pressure. Too far away and techniques are severely diminished because of a lack of leverage from the elbow.

> **For a visual demonstration, go to YouTube and search: "Live Life Like a Kung Fu Master—William Moy, Proper Elbow Position (Not Jammed Up)."**

Another fundamental technique is *wu sau*, the "guarding hand" or "protecting hand." It is a technique used mainly for blocking. Place the vertically extended hand approximately five to six inches from your sternum on the center line, with the wrist pushing forward and the straightened, tightly aligned fingers pulling back to create a tension (the thumb is tucked in).

Like the *tan sau* and *fuk sau*, if your *wu sau* is too close to your body it will collapse. You can easily test it this way: Begin to bring your *wu sau* closer to your sternum an eighth of an inch at a time. At each new interval, slap at its structure hard toward your body with your free hand. When the distance is within its correct boundary, your *wu sau* shouldn't budge, offering a strong resistance. When it ultimately falters (collapsing inward), you've positioned it too close.

Live Life Like a Kung Fu Master

FROM MY LIFE: AN EXTENSION OF THE EARTH

Kung Fu practitioners are pleased to borrow the power of the earth beneath us all. Imagine if the only thing separating two otherwise equal opponents was that one was efficiently using the ground for leverage and stability and the other was not. A similar application can be seen at sea. Watch an experienced captain walk across the deck of their ship in the midst of a rolling tide. Their steps will undoubtedly be strong, even, and forthright. Then compare that to the weak and unsteady steps of a greenhorn, someone with limited time at sea. The difference in stability would be astounding.

In this vein, my father once told me the story of when his teacher, Ip Man, took him and several other students to a Kung Fu event attended by many schools and sifus. One of the presenters there demonstrated a technique that he referred to as the "iron horse stance," with one leg positioned slightly in front of the other. He proudly proclaimed that no one in attendance could lift his front leg off the ground. He had trained this special stance for many years, causing his leg to become incredibly strong and heavy, like iron. The challenge didn't go unanswered. But while many eager people from the audience tried, none of them could succeed in lifting his leg.

Ip Man's students turned to him, asking if their sifu could disturb the man's stance. The master replied with a wry smile that he most likely could, if he were allowed to strike the practitioner (perhaps pondering a kick to the shin or groin). The students beamed at Ip Man's sense of humor and honesty.

After letting his students think about it overnight, the next day at lunch, Ip Man explained what they had witnessed. The presenter was really borrowing the power of the earth, to which he had affixed his stance. Imagine a U-shaped piece of steel with both ends resting on the ground. Only this piece of steel, in the form of two legs, was actually alive and reactive. Whenever you

Structure and Position

tried to lift up one end, your force would be transferred into the ground through the other end.

By creating such a sturdy structure, the ability to withstand significant loads becomes immense. This is something a Kung Fu practitioner can achieve with the legs, hips, and elbows—often the three in conjunction—forming a triangle that can defend against diverse types of powerful attacks.

> *The main thing about Bruce Lee is that he was a little guy . . . his quickness, his aggressiveness, his explosive power . . . all these things have to do with discipline and structure. He was able to go against the biggest guy, regardless of who he was.*
> —Evander Holyfield, Olympic gold medalist and professional heavyweight boxing champion

BY OTHER MEANS

Kung Fu comes in many forms. Defusing situations and disarming others doesn't always depend on a physical technique (such as a *bong sau*). Often, we build these same types of advantages and strengths for ourselves through other means in an effort to diminish the effects of unwanted outside forces upon our lives. Below are some common examples and possible solutions.

Perhaps a supervisor at your job regularly speaks to you in an unprofessional manner. How can you put yourself in a stronger position to address and combat this? Yes, you can certainly file a complaint with your company's human resources department. By all means. But you can also construct your own safeguards. Maybe it's possible to have your next interaction with that supervisor in the company of one or multiple coworkers, serving both as buffers and witnesses. You can also inform the supervisor that you'd prefer to take contemporaneous notes, or perhaps even use

[57]

the recorder app on your cell phone during your next discussion. That way you won't forget or misinterpret any of the instructions given to you. It's a way to impress upon your supervisor that what has become a normal course of business for them is no longer acceptable.

If you take mass transportation to school or work—especially at rush hour, be it in the morning or early evening—you'll eventually have an interaction with someone who will make you uncomfortable. It may be a look cast your way, a disregard for your personal space, or even an insistence in starting a conversation. Picking up and moving yourself is probably the best option, but that might not always be feasible on a crowded bus or train. So consider using a strategically placed umbrella, book bag, briefcase, knapsack, or garment slung over your arm as a space creator to give you greater distance from the problem. Other people standing around you can be used as makeshift barriers as well. And don't forget, possibly while your reading these pages, many people use open books to thwart unwanted conversations.

Structuring words into meaningful verbal cues can put us in better positions, often faster than anything else. *Don't do that. You're making me uncomfortable. Please, leave me alone.* These phrases do not characterize the speaker as weak. In fact, speaking your mind is a clear sign of assertiveness. Increasing your volume to alert others in the area and sharpening your tone of voice when needed can also be valuable tools.

Through your social, school, work, and travel experiences, you've most likely developed a good amount of natural Kung Fu. If your antenna is up and tingling, telling you that something is wrong about a particular situation, you should respect that feeling. Don't just ignore it. Your main course of action should be to promptly react by reestablishing yourself in a better position.

Structure and Position

NATURAL KUNG FU: LOOKING UP AT EVEN TALLER TREES

A two-time NBA Champion and MVP, Dave Cowens played center for the Boston Celtics from 1970 to 1980. Though Cowens stood *only* 6-foot-9 and weighed 230 pounds, he was actually undersized at the center position for the NBA. Cowens was routinely matched up against significantly taller players, some with wider frames, including Hall of Famers Wilt Chamberlain (7-foot-1, 275 lbs.), Kareem Abdul-Jabbar (7-foot-2), Bill Walton (6-foot-11), and Moses Malone (6-foot-10, 260 lbs.) to name a few. So how did Cowens compete so successfully night after night at the position? Aside from his incredible athletic talent and an inner drive to succeed, Dave Cowens was a master at holding superior on-court position and using body structure to gain an advantage.

"You have to know how and where to make contact, which usually only lasts for a few seconds. How to use your body isometrics, while keeping balance and control," noted Cowens, who was enshrined in the Naismith Memorial Basketball Hall of Fame in 1991. "Positioning also means how much room do you want between someone else's body and your own, both giving and then taking away space is vital . . . For example, I don't want to get rebounds from directly underneath the basket. I'd rather control a space three or four feet from the rim, giving myself more territory . . . It's also about the fundamentals of moving your feet and using your hips to create leverage."

Cowens may not be a trained martial artist, but his thoughts on how to properly use positioning and structure to gain an advantage is a close reflection of Kung Fu's center line theory.

"I call it being centered, playing from the middle of the court. As the anchor there, you can see everything going on around you, and you can move to either side, left or right, to respond in the shortest amount of time. That gives you an overall presence of always being able to get in an opponent's way. I believe the ability to create a powerful response comes from the center, from the middle of you."

The champion's assessment of how to excel on the court seemingly also applies to life.

"It's the three Cs for sure," said Cowens. "They are Concentration, Consistency, and Confidence—and knowing what you can do, and how hard you've worked to prepare yourself to do it, will bring even more confidence."

LIFE APPLICATIONS

- You're walking on a crowded and congested city sidewalk with people heading in both directions. Behind you, you're pulling a small cart filled with groceries. That's when you decide to push the cart in front of you, instead of pulling it from behind. Almost magically, a clear path opens in front of you, as people walking in the opposite direction see your cart and naturally step aside.
- You've tweaked a muscle in your back that's been slow to heal. So instead of doing push-ups with your body parallel to the ground, you do them on an inclined angle while leaning upon a chair, lessening the load on that muscle.
- While waiting at a bus stop in a neighborhood challenged by street crime, you start up a conversation with the person waiting beside you in order to give the impression to passersby that you're not alone.
- As your puppy has matured into a full-grown dog, the pulling by her on your daily walks has become harder to control. So you decide to attend a training session at a local park to become familiar with effectively and appropriately heel-walking your dog.

Structure and Position

What we observe as material bodies and forces are nothing but shapes and variations in the structure of space.
—Erwin Schrödinger, the father of quantum mechanics

CHAPTER SIX

MAINTAINING BALANCE AND FINDING A HORSE

Life is like riding a bicycle. To keep your balance, you must keep moving.

—Albert Einstein

BALANCE IS AN INCREDIBLY important attribute to success in almost any venue. Without it, we fight ourselves as much as the opponent, with gravity having its daunting say as well.

PHYSICAL ATTRIBUTES

Without proper balance, you can neither defend yourself nor attack an opponent with any real prowess. How can I achieve proper balance in my Kung Fu? Well, just like achieving balance in life, the answer is diligence. Balance is something on which you must work and practice to have true consistency. In fact, Kung Fu practitioners would prefer not to throw a strike at an opponent who, at that moment, is in control of their own balance. We

Live Life Like a Kung Fu Master

would much rather disrupt the opponent's balance first, compromising their ability to defend, before striking.

Two evenly matched opponents, both in possession of their balance, should be able to defend against each other's techniques, resulting in a theoretical stalemate and, therefore, a lot of wasted energy. Not what we're trying to achieve in a martial art based on efficiency, such as Wing Chun.

Yes, poor balance can render your techniques ineffective. But the reverse is also true. Using a poorly formed technique can also negatively affect your balance, especially if you get jammed up, with an opponent owning your critical distance, and your toes come off the floor. So in combat, the two—good balance and a properly formed technique—are quite intertwined.

You should first concentrate on building and improving your balance through training exercises. Initially, you should begin with static exercises, and then integrate training while in motion. Static exercises include doing *Siu Nim Tao* until it becomes an innate part of your being. This form teaches us to keep our shoulders square, back straight, and pelvis tucked beneath the spine, preventing us from leaning forward. At some point, you can even try performing *Siu Nim Tao* on one leg, which is aptly referred to as a "rooster stance," mimicking the freestanding fowl.

Your balance will also be aided by developing a strong horse stance, as if you were straddling a horse, while lowering your center of gravity to increase the pressure on the legs. In training a deep horse stance, sinking lower and lower, trying to hold the stance for as long as you can (if not performing *Siu Nim Tao*), make sure to be doing something with your hands as well. For example, throwing punches on the center line will test your ability to remain balanced and not lean forward in the direction of the energy you've just released.

To work on your balance while in motion, place your hands in *jong sau*, the basic on guard position. If you don't have a

Maintaining Balance and Finding a Horse

training partner, begin to shadow an imaginary opponent, always keeping your guard pointed at the opponent's center. Slide your feet—which should never lose contact with the floor—to continually face the opponent. Switching lead hands, changing from the right to the left, will give you a bit of added momentum to help secure your balance.

For a visual demonstration, go to YouTube and search: "Live Life Like a Kung Fu Master—William Moy, Balance in Motion/Jong Sau."

Many students who've studied other arts or competed at sports such as tennis, basketball, football, and wrestling ask me about weight distribution and their balance. They want to know if they should keep their weight distributed fifty-fifty or sixty-forty between their front and back leg. My father never liked dealing in such percentages because he felt that it made the process of balance too technical. And I agree.

True balance is achieved when the pressure center of your feetis located in the middle of your soles. To facilitate this, it is important to use your knees effectively. The degree to which you bend your knees determines the distribution of weight on your feet. More bending of the knees will shift added weight toward the front of your foot, while less bending will result in added weight on your heel. Remember, balance is something that is ever shifting and changing. That's why we need to be so diligent and observant in our approach to maintain it.

FROM MY LIFE: OVER EAGER

During my early years of training under my father's tutelage, I eagerly awaited graduating to a stage where I could use my Kung Fu in motion (instead of just static exercises). It's something that confronts every beginner: the accelerated desire to perform what they perceive to be the "real" Kung Fu. In other arts such as boxing, taekwondo, karate, and jiu-jitsu, novices are right in the mix, training and even sparring early on in their education. But not so in Wing Chun, as you need to first change your mindset and physical reaction from force to feelings.

Finally, my time came. I was allowed to enter a new stage in training called *Tui Ma*, which means "pushing horse." Your training partner isn't pushing you off your spot with strength, but rather with their polished techniques and timing. Lacking their overall experience, I was unable to control and defend my center through the same techniques. They were moving me around, pushing me off my horse as if I were a rag doll. All because I hadn't yet mastered the combination of maintaining a good balance with a strong horse nor the proper techniques to secure my center.

My confidence was somewhat shattered. Had this been a stage I wanted to reach for so long? Something for which I had practically begged my father?

Today, I often see the same reaction in my students when they graduate to *Tui Ma*. The look in their eyes of suddenly being completely lost and dominated, as if all of their hard work up until that point had been meaningless. It can be a look that communicates the worrisome thought, *Maybe I don't have what it takes to succeed in Kung Fu?*

That's why, before I move a student onto this stage, I have a conversation with them. I will explain exactly what it's going to be like, bringing together everything they've learned with something totally new. How they may have to reevaluate their progress by going back to basics to clean up their shortcomings.

If a student is going to suddenly stop coming to class and walk away from the time they put into learning the art, it usually happens during *Tui Ma*.

Maintaining Balance and Finding a Horse

As for me, my father was the patriarch of his own Kung Fu family, so I wasn't going anywhere . . . not unless I was to run away from home to join the circus. And, most likely, my balance wasn't nearly good enough for that, either.

In the end, I went back to *Siu Nim Tao* to improve my horse stance, understanding how it needed to be activated to come to life, to apply its strengths while in motion. I started doing its opening section even slower, taking more than twenty minutes with the *tan sau* and *fuk sau*, letting an entire stick of incense burn down with each repetition. It was like climbing the mountain all over again. But that committed process brought me to where I wanted to go. First, getting a handle on *Tui Ma* and, eventually, progressing beyond it.

> *Focus on being balanced—success is balance.*
> —Laila Ali, female boxing champion and daughter
> of Muhammad Ali

LIFE AND CHANGING WINDS

No one expects you to suddenly develop the balance of a tightrope walker, navigating a thin wire strung between two skyscrapers without a safety net below. That's an extreme. But balance is among Kung Fu's core concepts, and studying the art will more than likely improve that attribute in you. The hope is that it will inspire you to refine the balance in other parts of your life as well.

For example, many of us have a tough time balancing our professional and personal lives. With more people working from a home office since the COVID-19 pandemic, our work-life balance can become somewhat blurred at times. Does a forty-five-minute lunch break dovetail into a two-mile walk with your dog on a beautiful day when you don't want to be inside? Does having your computer on the kitchen island mean the lure of finishing

Live Life Like a Kung Fu Master

that final sales report has put you an hour behind schedule in preparing dinner for a hungry family? Will you continue to be eating a balanced diet, or will the upcoming coming holiday meals with extended family throw your best efforts into total disarray? How about your retirement portfolio? Is it properly balanced for the long haul with a small array of fluid stocks, but many more stable bonds? Or will that new investment podcast tempt you into more risky allocations?

And, most importantly, will you be able to lean on family and friends through the hardest of times, giving you balance when you need it most?

Want to see balance in action? Watch any football game and wait for the offense to come to the line of scrimmage in an unbalanced line, usually overloading the right or left side with more blocking power. It will be just a few seconds before the ball is snapped to the quarterback and the play is in motion. That's how long the defense has to adjust, bringing balance back to their own scheme.

Of course, you'll need to keep your eye on that tightrope walker, too. Plenty of adjustments will need to be made whenever an unexpectedly heavy wind kicks up.

NATURAL KUNG FU: SKY WALKER

Denis Josselin is one of the world's great tightrope walkers. So you'd naturally believe that balance would come easily to the French-born athlete. Not so. "The inner ear is one of the centers of balance. I'm deaf in one ear and hard of hearing in the other. As a result, I have no balance. When I stand on one foot, I fall," noted Josselin. "I'm not working on balance. I'm playing with my imbalances. Strength, respect, and a better view of oneself lies in accepting one's weaknesses, not in emphasizing one's so-called abilities."

Maintaining Balance and Finding a Horse

Josselin has been training newcomers to walking a wire for more than two decades. How does he coach them? "I get them to work on their breathing, their mind, and their positivity. The hardest thing for these people is to disconnect from their brain (and overthinking), to reconnect with their instinct and trust it. Simple breathing and visualization exercises can de-stress, relieve tension, restore calm, and energize. Positivity through the transformation of inhibiting [negative] thoughts, when practiced regularly, can achieve a great deal in both mental and physical terms."

As in Kung Fu, the concept of structure is incredibly important to the tightrope walker. Not only in keeping their own body structure perfect as they're perched upon the wire, but the structure of the equipment as well. "Above all, there's time needed for technical aspects; how to ensure that all the installations can withstand the multiple mechanical forces, and find sufficiently strong anchoring points on the buildings. For example, what equipment will I need? What rope will I use? How many meters of guy wires [ropes installed perpendicular to the walking rope used for stabilization] will I need?" said Josselin, who also practices Chinese *Qigong* (*chee-gong*) exercises, based on the martial arts principle of connecting mind, body and spirit.

What is Josselin's focus like when he's actually walking the wire, high above the crowds? "For a tightrope walker to be successful, his concentration must be at its peak. He must be in a state of sublime grace, at over 200 percent of his abilities. The tightrope walker has to be there, present, as calm and reassuring as possible. It's all about inner strength, mental strength. They have to be a lightning rod for any negative energies. They have no right to negative thoughts or doubts. They must be totally in the moment, aware of the risks, remaining humble and positive to fight against the arrogance of ego."

Live Life Like a Kung Fu Master

PAUL'S PERSPECTIVE: REAL-LIFE JENGA?

Ever wondered what it would be like to play a game of Jenga against a Kung Fu master? You know, the game comprised of stacking fifty-four small wooden blocks, each one three times as long as it is wide, and one-fifth as thick as its length. When British board game designer Leslie Scott invented Jenga (a Swahili word meaning "to build") back in 1983, she probably wasn't considering what someone so steeped in personal balance, such as a martial artist, could bring to the game.

The taller it got, would a Kung Fu master's wooden tower waver less because of their martial arts skills? Would balance, touch, and feel be totally on their side, making them incredibly hard to defeat? It's an interesting thought for debate.

But if a master could transfer their martial skills to the game, they would still face the same quandaries we all do. You see, no one can actually play the game alone. Just like in life, we must consider the actions of others in relation to our own.

If our Jenga opponent makes what we would consider to be a bad move, yet the tower doesn't topple, it becomes incumbent upon us to deal with a tenuous situation. It can happen that same away in life: on the street, at school, work, or home. The actions of someone else can put our balance, physically and mentally, in extremely challenging circumstances, which can pop up at any moment.

That's the test of the game, and the test of life for everyone, whether you've taken the time to hone and bolster your balance or not.

LIFE APPLICATIONS

- You've tried for months to correctly balance a photo hanging on a single hook upon the wall of your living room, but it seems like every other day the photo tilts and you

have tostraighten it. Finally, you decide to add a second hook for increased support, and have not had to address the situation since.
- It's your company's busy season, and you've been working close to sixty hours a week for the past two months. You've even taken it upon yourself to start working weekends. As a result, you've become increasingly short-tempered at home. That's when your significant other sits you down for a serious talk about finding a more appropriate balance in your life between work and family.
- After knee surgery, you use a cane for several weeks to keep you well balanced, free from falls, and from possibly reinjuring the knee.
- The best part of your tennis game is your powerful serve. So when it comes time for you to choose a partner for the local doubles tournament, you pick someone who has a skill set that perfectly complements yours, creating a balanced duo: a player with a solid forehand and backhand volley.

When I'm listening, I'm looking for a balance that you could see in anything. Whether it's a great painting or a building or a sunset.
　　　　　—Rick Rubin, record producer and executive

KAYLA HARRISON: SHUTTING OUT THE NOISE
Ohio native Kayla Harrison is a professional mixed martial artist. Prior to turning pro, she won a pair of gold medals in judo, one at the 2012 Olympics in London and a second at the 2016 Olympics in Rio. The Japanese art of judo translates as the "gentle

(continued next page)

Live Life Like a Kung Fu Master

way," with maintaining your balance while attacking the balance of your opponent being a key to success.

"Judo players are capable of controlling themselves in almost any situation. Because of the rigorous training and all the work I do, it's really hard to off-balance me in life," noted Harrison, who as a survivor of sexual assault has started The Fearless Foundation to help others find their best footing on the road to recovery.

In the 78 kg gold medal match at the 2012 Olympics in London, it was the voices of the spectators in attendance that attempted to off-balance Kayla in her pursuit of victory. She was pitted against crowd favorite Gemma Gibbons, a native Londoner who grew up just several miles from the venue where the two combatants were facing off. "Gemma! Gemma!" the audience shouted in support of their hometown hero. But the pinpoint focus of Kayla Harrison had blocked out virtually every decibel of outside distraction. Intent on controlling the pace of the match and keeping her opponent off-balance, Harrison's rhythm subtly changed from moderate to slow, slow to fast and several variations in between, waiting for an opening in which she could turn relatively supersonic.

"The name of the game is finding your openings and seizing upon them. If you try to force things, you'll use too much energy. For me, judo is a finesse sport, the art of using your opponent's momentum against them. Change the velocity of moves. Change the speed. Then, when there's an opening, explode and hopefully get a beautiful throw," said Harrison. That's exactly what the then twenty-two-year-old Olympian did to her advantage. Harrison defeated Gibbons, 2–0, with a pair of lightning-quick, momentum-driven techniques, one early in the contest and another inside the final ninety seconds of the four-minute match, becoming the first-ever American judo player to stand atop the podium and hear the US national anthem.

CHAPTER SEVEN

DISTANCE AWARENESS AND ANGLES

One sees qualities at a distance and defects at close range.
                    —Victor Hugo, French writer and politician

KNOWING HOW TO MARTIAL (analyze and dictate) distance will help create appropriate boundaries in your life. Whether that distance between the situations, opportunities, and people in question shrinks or grows, should always depend on your well-informed observations.

PHYSICAL ATTRIBUTES

A staple that connects many different and diverse martial arts is the concept of distance, and it is absolutely at the core of Wing Chun Kung Fu. For decades, students have asked me: "Sifu, at what point do I need to defend myself?" "When should I decide to strike or kick someone?"

Live Life Like a Kung Fu Master

The answer is fairly straightforward: defense/offense occurs whenever someone who poses an immediate threat to you enters your critical distance. How is your critical distance determined? Simply extend both arms out in front of you. Several inches past your fingertips should be considered the outermost edge of your critical distance to be struck with a punch. But if your attacker is considerably taller than you, extend this distance by another few inches. No one who means to do you harm should ever come into that space with a "free pass." It is a patch of ground that they need to earn.

Understanding your critical distance and other relevant distances is referred to as distance awareness, something you will need to work on and ultimately refine to strengthen your overall Kung Fu. This includes combatants moving into your range, as well as you moving out of range to prevent being attacked. Remember, the critical distance for you kicking someone, or you being kicked, is normally extended by approximately eighteen inches past the punch/strike zone, since the leg is longer than the arm.

You will often fill a good portion of your critical distance with your *jong sau*, our on-guard position, instructing intruders to, "Stay back!" Opponents attempting to get close enough to you—perhaps even with a cocked fist—to throw a punch that can reach your body may actually walk into your ready-to-strike hands. Or the opponent, suffering from poor distance awareness, might judge your extended guard as your body, beginning their strike from several feet away. Yes, in this scenario, they will be throwing the first punch. However, they have not yet breached your critical distance, and this will give you the time and opportunity to change the angle, usually moving yourself just outside of their strike.

Why is changing angles so important to your Kung Fu? It gives you the opportunity to assume a very powerful position—one in which your attacker is squarely on your center line, while

[74]

you are not occupying the attacker's center line. From that far superior angle, you'll have every chance to subdue the threat quickly and thoroughly.

For a visual demonstration, go to YouTube and search: *"Live Life Like a Kung Fu Master—William Moy, Critical Distance/Changing Angles"*

FROM MY LIFE: UNEXPECTED ENCOUNTER

During my younger days, I enjoyed going out at night on the weekends. At the time, like many people my age, I frequented dance and music clubs in New York City. And though I don't particularly have a taste for alcohol and rarely consume it, I do like being around people having a good time—especially my friends—and sharing a party atmosphere with them.

Of course, traveling to and from different neighborhoods late at night brings its own set of challenges. Neighborhoods vary in their ability to keep residents and visitors safe on the streets. You have to consider the crime rate, drug usage, and even street gangs when walking through a section of the city with which you are not very familiar. And boosting the potential negativity of that equation, I would normally be there under the cover of darkness,

On one such night, I had just left a club and was walking alone to retrieve my parked car. The sidewalk was relatively empty ahead of me as I spotted a man coming in my direction. He was staggering a bit and seemed unsteady, as if he might be intoxicated. I dismissed him as harmless. But when I came within arm's reach of him, he suddenly grabbed the lapel of my jacket. His other hand was buried inside a pocket. He told me that he had a weapon before shouting, "Give me all your money!"

Despite my years of training in Kung Fu, I had made the classic mistake of allowing this stranger, in a place and time where I

Live Life Like a Kung Fu Master

should have been much more guarded, into my critical distance, close enough to compromise me.

In the midst of that glaring mistake, however, I quickly refocused myself. Understanding that he couldn't hit me with the hand locked onto my lapel, I focused on the hand concealed inside his pocket. I remained poised to strike at his face, still uncertain as to whether he actually had a weapon. Fortunately, with just a few words, I managed to convince him that I was ready to comply with his demand.

Once he let go of my lapel, I leaped back, reestablishing a safe distance to defend an unarmed attack. But I still had to consider that he might have a knife or even a firearm. So I started to run, and he decided to chase me. That's when I headed directly into the middle of street, vocalizing what was going on for others to hear and take notice. In a sense, more eyes and ears on the situation meant increased safety.

I was fast, but so was my assailant. Not wanting to have an obscured view, I turned to face him. With adrenaline pumping through me, I took a defensive stance, raising my hands in the *jong sau* guard position and yelled, "Come on!"

Thankfully, the man abruptly changed direction and ran away down the street.

When I was finally sitting inside my locked car, I critiqued myself. Yes, I had lost control of my critical distance. That was a hard-learned lesson but I was quickly able to reestablish that distance by remaining calm and relying on my training. I wasn't exactly pleased with myself, but I could live with the outcome.

The very next night, I decided to stay home.

> *The shortest distance between two points is under construction.*
>
> —Leo Aikman, historian and journalist

Distance Awareness and Angles

WEEKEND WARRIORS

Suppose you're jogging down the street. A half-block up ahead of you, someone is holding a small dog on a leash. The person with the dog is talking to someone else and doesn't notice that you're approaching . . . but the dog certainly sees you coming, and appears very excited. The dog lets out a *yap*, and the owner tightens their grip on the leash. The traffic in the street is heavy, so shifting over to the blacktop is not an option. You're in a good running rhythm and you'd prefer not to slow down, so you begin to study the length of the leash. You've encountered this dog before and you already know that it's a leaper with sharp nails. And this morning, you're barelegged, clad in running shorts. Will you make it past with your legs unscathed? Cut it just close enough to give the dog a deserving pat on the head as you jog past? Or will you later be applying antiseptic to your legs to deal with the multiple scratches? Well, it all depends on your ability to properly judge distance.

Perhaps you're a really good hitter for your company softball team. In fact, for the past two seasons you've led the local commercial league in home runs. However, this year, your homers have been at a minimum. You're undercutting the ball on nearly every swing, with the thought of gaining more lift to send one over the outfield fence. But the margin for error is small in using such an increased launch angle, and you're hitting infield popups at an alarming rate. So your team's coach approaches you with a suggestion to substantially lower the angle of your swing. By doing this you'll hit more line drives, which can easily carry for home runs, and pop up much less.

Or consider this: an all-star pickleball player you're not. However, your Kung Fu training has given you a solid understanding of distance and angles. You're playing doubles and the other team's super server is cutting the ball at a sharp angle to the left. Your partner, who has been struggling to return those serves, is playing too far beyond the baseline and a half step to the right. So you call a quick time out, instructing your partner to take two steps forward and one to the left, providing a better solution to address the ratio of distance to angle for that incoming serve. Now that's teamwork!

NATURAL KUNG FU: PAYING ATTENTION

Lea Page has an incredible Kung Fu eye for detail, especially when she's out walking. In her sixties, Lea lives in the Big Sky state of Montana and walks two to seven miles a day. Of course, on those rather routine walks her mind might wander a bit to the needs of her family or any number of daily chores yet to be accomplished. But for Lea, walking in new surroundings means intensely focusing, being in the present, and observing every detail.

In 2022, Lea traveled from the US to France to walk a thousand-mile trail . . . alone! It's referred to as the Via Francigena, a path that spans from Canterbury to Rome and Santa Maria di Leuca.

"It took me two months to complete, walking approximately twenty miles per day, from early in the morning to about two or three in the afternoon, before it got too hot," said Lea, who had previously completed a similar solo trek in Spain.

What was at the core of taking such a journey?

"It was about noticing and paying attention. And when you really pay attention, you discover there's a lot going on," she noted. "Everything you see and hear is new. So you're focused on taking it all in and not thinking. It was probably the longest amount of time in my life that I was completely in the present, without my mind wandering to something like a shopping list."

As a woman, was there fear of traveling alone along some desolate paths in a foreign country?

"There was definitely some fear, but not the way you might think. I was terrified about going the wrong way," said Lea. "As far as being a woman and walking alone—that's life for a woman. I grew up in Washington, DC, and coming home from a night shift waitressing job during high school to save up for college, I learned to project that 'don't mess with me' walk."

Lea is currently planning future long-distance walks in new environments, again with the plan to be completely zoned-in on every potential detail.

PAUL'S PERSPECTIVE: DISTANCE, TIME, AND A BETTER ANGLE

It was our weekly basketball game, comprised of a strong core of players who had been competing against each other for over a decade. One of those players, an extremely nice guy and someone I considered a friend, had been battling severe anger issues. If there was to be a fight or yelling match on the court, the odds were good that he would be involved.

On this night, Angry Bob showed up after having a few beers. Whoever made the sides for that singular game did it with their heart and not their head, because one team had far superior players to the other. Angry Bob was on the side that was losing by a lopsided score, and he was getting angrier with every basket by the opposing team (of which I was a part).

Angry Bob began pushing and shoving with one of my teammates while going up and down the court. It got really nasty and I was convinced the pair would soon come to blows.

"We're only fighting because you're losing," my teammate, who'd been involved in the intensely brewing fracas, snapped at him.

That's when Angry Bob proclaimed, "I've had enough of you. I'm going to guard Paul instead."

I was thrilled to hear it. Now we could finish this one-sided game and avoid the impending brawl. A second later, Angry Bob, who was now standing in front of me, looked up at the sky and

Live Life Like a Kung Fu Master

shouted, "I'm not going to take this anymore!" To my astonishment, he decided to throw that punch, which had been welling up inside of him . . . at me.

I had seen so many crisp punches while training under Sifu William that Angry Bob's punch seemed slow and sloppy. Despite the fact that he was already inside my critical distance—something that routinely happens when you're playing sports—I sidestepped it and was now standing just off his shoulder, with Angry Bob on my center line and my return punch already in motion.

In the fraction of a second before my fist contacted his face, I felt bad about returning fire on my somewhat intoxicated friend. So, at the last instant, I opened my hand and palmed him high on the neck. He flew back seven or eight feet before falling to the floor.

He then jumped up and charged right back at me, settling just a foot or so outside of my raised *jong sau*. This is the problem with pulling back on a punch and going easy on an attacker: you now might have to win superior position all over again to defend yourself.

He was wild with anger, only I refused to show any real emotion. I just focused on his body as a whole with a blank look on my face, waiting for him to move first. That's when someone decided to put the basketball back into play, and my team immediately scored the winning basket.

Angry Bob never made that move toward me to reengage. Instead, he walked off the court to a nearby bench. There he took a seat and started cursing at me. For the next several minutes he rumbled like a seething volcano about to explode.

I kept my distance, probably forty feet from him, still standing on the court.

Then I waited and waited for Angry Bob to run out of steam. He verbally threatened and cursed me for nearly five minutes, using the most profane language and images you could imagine, until it eventually came to a halt.

[80]

Distance Awareness and Angles

That's when I shelved my pride and approached him on the bench.

"I'm sorry about this," I conveyed in a calm voice. "I should have never put my hands on you. I know this was all about you being angry at that other guy. It had nothing to do with me."

"That's alright, Paulie," he said, getting up to leave. "Thanks, I accept your apology."

Sometimes reality needs to be re-envisioned to avoid serious and long-lasting conflict.

If I displayed a modicum of good Kung Fu in that encounter, it was in keeping my distance from Angry Bob as he raged uncontrollably on the bench, waiting for that extended moment to pass, and then changing my angle to address the situation with some soothing and probably unexpected words. Plus, at the end of the day, even though he was definitely in the wrong, my apologizing further diffused the situation and allowed us all to move on.

LIFE APPLICATIONS

- Your community has a split opinion about a homeless shelter being newly opened on Main Street. You're personally unsure of where you stand on the issue, so you accept an offer to meet with some of the shelter's caretakers, hoping it will give you a better perspective.
- You see approaching thunder clouds and then a flash of lightning. Five seconds later you hear the echoing thunder. Remembering the "five seconds per mile" rule from science class, you know that the center of the storm is still approximately a distance of one mile away—not yet encroaching upon your critical distance and immediate safety.
- Most municipalities deem it illegal to park within a fifteen-foot distance of a fire hydrant. That way firefighters can have room to access the hydrant in an emergency.

In reality, they are securing a critical distance to respond without obstructions.
- Many businesses pivoted during the pandemic, changing the angles in which they reached and serviced their consumers.

Look at situations from all angles, and you will become more open.

—Dalai Lama

ANOTHER TRIO OF NEW TECHNIQUES
In order to fully understand the Kung Fu exercises in the upcoming chapter, you'll need to be versed on an additional trio of fundamental techniques.

Pak sau (slapping hand) normally comes quite naturally to novices, as blocking is something we've been doing most of our lives. In Wing Chun, we use the palm of the hand, often cupped, to block an attack, moving an incoming strike just off the center line and past our body. It is usually applied or contacted just above the attacker's wrist, or even directly on the elbow for some particular applications. The *pak sau* appears at the end of the first section of *Siu Nim Tao*.

Lop sau (grabbing hand) is applied by grabbing an arm, again, normally just above the wrist, before pulling it downward and often off-center, disrupting the attacker's balance. After the grab and subsequent pull, we always let go of the appendage in order to be free to attack and defend with both our hands.

Jut sau (deflecting hand) is a short and sharp deflecting technique, which is often born from a *fuk sao*. The aligned fingers are raised vertically, creating a downward tension in the wrist that can stop and anchor several incoming techniques, including punches. It resembles a *wu sau* once fully formed.

Distance Awareness and Angles

Jut Sau

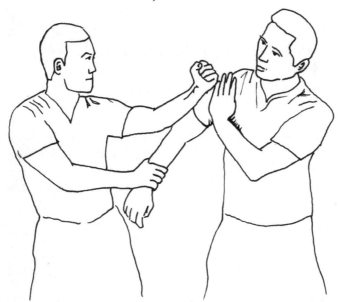

Lop Sau

[83]

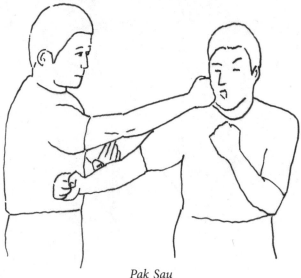

Pak Sau

For a visual demonstration, go to YouTube and search: "Live Life Like a Kung Fu Master—William Moy, Pak Sau. Lop Sau and Jut Sau."

HONORED GUEST: SIFU LEO IMAMURA (BRAZIL)

Sifu Leo Imamura has dedicated his life to the art of Kung Fu, sharing his knowledge by word and example. Imamura's journey, however—especially at the start— was anything but a straight line. He grew up in Brazil, the eldest son of Japanese descendants who consistently preached the value of education to their children.

"I grew up playing soccer. After all, it was Brazil. But my nerves hindered my performance, so I turned to martial arts, studying judo and karate. Only those arts didn't suit my personality," said Sifu Imamura. "Then I found Kung Fu, and that really helped me to relax. Also, I was just an average athlete. Kung Fu

(continued next page)

Distance Awareness and Angles

emphasized timing over speed, and using the opponent's own power against them. Eventually, I decided to become a professional martial artist. I had already gone through five years of studying law at the university level when I broke the news to my parents. To their credit, and reflecting the overwhelming love they had for their children, they supported my decision."

Imamura decided to study Wing Chun in Hong Kong. But the most affordable flight from Brazil to the Far East brought him through New York City, where he was being shown around by the older brother of his Brazilian-based martial arts teacher, an airline employee who lived in New York and helped to facilitate the young man's trip.

"We went to Manhattan's Chinatown to visit a well-known martial arts store. Continuing on our journey, we saw a sign that read Moy Yat Kung Fu. My guide recognized Moy Yat's name, so we walked up the six flights to the school, unannounced."

As providence would have it, Sifu Moy Yat, his wife Helen, and their seventeen-year-old son, William, were all in attendance at the school, with the Saturday morning class having concluded an hour or so earlier.

"It was almost like the family was waiting for me to arrive," Imamura continued. "I remember that we had some conversation, and Sifu Moy Yat told me that if things didn't work out in Hong Kong, he'd accept me as his student. He must have planted some seeds of good Kung Fu during that brief meeting, because after studying for a while in Hong Kong, I knew in my heart that New York was where I needed to be."

Imamura went on to study for fourteen years under Moy Yat, splitting his time between living in Brazil and taking numerous extended trips to New York, where he initially slept in the school before being invited to share space in the family's Brooklyn apartment.

(continued next page)

Live Life Like a Kung Fu Master

"Sifu Moy Yat displayed a lot of patience with me as a student, teaching both the physical and mental aspects of the art—especially how to live a life based in Kung Fu. That's what he emphasized to me most, a Kung Fu life. I remember he once said with a huge smile, "The art is so good you can even use it to fight," said Imamura, with a warm laugh.

The desire of Imamura's parents for their son to have a career in an academic field came true in 1992, when he was recognized as the first university professor of martial arts by the Education and Culture Ministry of Brazil. Since then, he has participated in several projects concerning various martial arts, with an emphasis on Kung Fu, throughout the country's university, high school, and primary school system.

"Universities have used my expertise in Kung Fu for students in their MBA programs. They believe that aspects of the art will help students to be better administrators, and they are correct in that idea," he noted. "I use the phrase 'martial intelligence' to describe it. The fighting or physical aspect of martial arts is just symbolic. During combat, the practitioner needs to be relaxed, paying attention to every surrounding detail, respecting their opponent, and feeling for when the door is opened to properly respond. These are the same qualities that I want all of my students to bring to their daily lives."

Ip Man and Moy Yat

Moy Yat painting

Moy Yat playing the Kwan

My father, Moy Yat

Me with Si Hing Rex and his sons, circa 1981.

A self-portrait playing the Wu Sau position.

Playing the Jong--always practicing!

Sifu William teaching his students.

Sifu William playing Chi Sau with one of his students.

Me practicing on the beach.

An amazing way to start the day!

CHAPTER EIGHT

A "System" of Kung Fu

Education is that whole system of human training
within and without the schoolhouse walls.
  —W.E.B. Du Bois, author, sociologist, and historian

SYSTEMS ARE STRUCTURE. WE often discover that creativity and systems go hand in hand. For the artist knows where the borders of the canvas are located. That frees the artist to concentrate solely on filling the available space, not defining the parameters. It's the same in life, with the sky acting as our border. We don't have wings to fly. Yet that never stopped anyone from soaring.

PHYSICAL ATTRIBUTES

In the world of martial arts, Wing Chun Kung Fu is considered a "system," and correctly so. In fact, that's one of its main strengths. It is estimated that nearly three million people worldwide practice the art. How did they learn? Because it's a system, with the

[87]

overwhelming majority of its practitioners learning through an almost identical pattern of steps, including several static core exercises and techniques accompanied by the opening form, *Siu Nim Tao*. Then their bourgeoning talents were brought into dynamic motion through succeeding forms and training exercises that are more free flowing.

Why is that congruity so important?

First, this building block training formula has proved nearly impeccable in developing a practitioner's skill set. Earlier in this text we discussed the axiom "Wing Chun Chuen Jing Tung," which translates as "Wing Chun authentically passing down." The reason that axiom is so praised is because the elemental order of the system is perfectly aligned, promoting complete and even-paced growth in an art where most beginning students need to learn that good technique can overcome size and strength.

Secondly, the systematic approach creates a common baseline for practitioners from different schools and families to share their experiences, compare, and even test their Kung Fu. Naturally, not every sifu teaches every exercise the exact same way. There may even be a minor variation in the order of exercises. However, a diligent Wing Chun student would be hard pressed to view a class in a different school and be totally confused by the lesson at hand.

NORMAL ORDER OF SYSTEMATIC EXERCISES

All of the exercises focus on the center line, either clearing or defending it.

Pak Sau Drill

Two practitioners stand face to face, with one throwing punches on the center line, alternating between their right and left hand. The other, the receiver in this case, blocks each incoming strike with a *pak sau*. The left hand blocks the incoming right-handed punch and the right hand blocks the left-handed punch.

A "System" of Kung Fu

Pak Da **Drill**

This builds upon the *pak sau* drill with the receiver now accomplishing two things, blocking and striking simultaneously with both hands. The receiver blocks the incoming punch, clearing the center line for the strike already in motion with the opposite hand. *Da* means "Strike."

> *For a visual demonstration, go to YouTube and search: "Live Life Like a Kung Fu Master—William Moy, Pak Sau and Pak Da Drill."*

Lop Sau **Drill**

A pair of practitioners standing face to face alternate between using a *bong sau* to defend and a *lop da* to attack, clearing the center line. This is a free-flowing exercise that begins the process of shifting from the right to left side, putting both arms into play at the discretion of the two participants.

> *For a visual demonstration, go to YouTube and search: "Live Life Like a Kung Fu Master—William Moy, Lop Sau Drill."*

Don Chi Sau

This serves as a limited introduction to the free-flowing exercise of *chi sau*, which we will discuss in depth in the following chapter. *Don chi sau* is a single-arm exercise, as opposed to the two arms used in *chi sau*. In this drill, a palm strike is neutralized with a *jut sau* by a practitioner who now controls the center line, immediately turning the *jut sau* position into a straight punch. The defending practitioner, who initiated the palm strike, defends the incoming punch with a *bong sau*, taking it offline.

Live Life Like a Kung Fu Master

For a visual demonstration, go to YouTube and search: "Live Life Like a Kung Fu Master—William Moy, Demonstrating Do Chi Sau."

Luk Sau

This "rolling hands" drill serves as another introduction to *chi sau* by adding additional limited energy as a pair of practitioners use wrist to wrist contact to simultaneously roll both arms—either from *tan sau* to *bong sau* (one arm), or *fuk sau* in two positions, going from high to low.

For a visual demonstration, go to YouTube and search: "Live Life Like a Kung Fu Master—William Moy, Demonstrating Luk Sau."

Tui Ma

We've previously discussed this "pushing horse" exercise in chapter Six, where the burgeoning practitioner gets their first experience at testing their horse stance under pressure, being pushed in a straight line by a more advanced partner. The hands of both participants are also rolling from one technique to another during this exercise.

For a visual demonstration, go to YouTube and search: "Live Life Like a Kung Fu Master—William Moy, Demonstrating Tui Ma."

FROM MY LIFE: IT'S ABOUT YOU, NOT ME

I rarely train one-on-one with my students, and there's a specific reason for that. I try to remain focused on teaching Wing Chun Kung Fu as a system, and not my personal interpretation of the art or my own individual style. After teaching for decades,

I understand that students will try to emulate their sifu, believing I must be the perfect representation of correct and good Kung Fu. And though most sifus serve as excellent role models for their students, copying your sifu—who most likely has a different body type and attributes—can actually stifle a student's growth in finding their own personal style.

I recall how a particularly stormy night produced a low turnout for class. Just five students attended on that rainy and windblown evening. So as the first four students trained in pairs, I partnered with the lone remaining student. We worked together for probably a half hour straight. That's when this student turned to me and made the observation, "I can see how small pieces of your skills are present in some of my classmates. But no one else here plays Kung Fu exactly the way you do."

Those words were music to my ears, striking a satisfied chord in me, before I added, "Or like each other."

Director Steven Spielberg once said, "The delicate balance of mentoring someone is not creating them in your own image, but giving them the opportunity to create themselves." And I have often equated that statement with my own teaching of Kung Fu.

While the terms "system" and "style" are sometimes used interchangeably, they carry distinct meanings in martial arts. A martial arts system refers to the overall framework of techniques, principles, and philosophies that form the foundation of a particular discipline. It encompasses the underlying structure and organization of the art and is often established by its founders or prominent practitioners. The system provides a cohesive approach to training, presenting a logical progression of skills and knowledge.

A martial arts style refers to the individual expression and interpretation of a particular system. It represents the unique characteristics and nuances that distinguish one practitioner from another.

Live Life Like a Kung Fu Master

Both system and style have their value and importance in martial arts. And sometimes it takes a small class on a rain-soaked night to reinforce that in a longtime sifu.

I don't love studying. I hate studying. I like learning. Learning is beautiful.
—Natalie Portman, Academy Award–winning actress

MALL WALKING/PUT IT IN DRIVE

How might a novice Kung Fu student feel? Overwhelmed is not unusual. You're learning both a new language and new body movements simultaneously, attempting to put it all together in your mind. That's why learning via a system, being grounded within a framework—one that older students who model for you have also traversed, becomes extremely valuable. You've probably had many experiences with people trying to speak a new language for the first time. Take English, for example; some learning the numerous conjugations can easily be frustrated. Just as you master the phrase "I have," you're thrown by the idea that it's "he has" and "she has."

It's like being in a huge mall for the very first time and trying to get your bearings.

You go over to one of the maps on display and discover that *you are here.* For the moment, you're a virtual X on a grid, trying to transfer that representation to a three-dimensional world. Next, you study the directory of stores to find the one that holds your initial interest—the reason you traveled here—is located on the third floor at the far end of the mall. There are also stairs, escalators, and elevators to consider. Without that map and the ability to systematically plot from Point A to Point B and beyond, your impending journey might feel more like an uncertain trek to nowhere.

A "System" of Kung Fu

Now think about the first time trying you went to get a driver's license. No one there actually asked you to drive right away. Instead, you moved through their systematic process. You sat static in a chair and took a written test with questions about road signs, hand signals, and the appropriate distance in car lengths between vehicles on the road. Passing that exam got you a learner's permit. And, in future practicing sessions, you could only be in motion behind the wheel with an experienced driver there to help guide you. Sounds like a Kung Fu student starting the "pushing horse" exercise, *tui ma*.

The fact that virtually every municipality in the US has basically the same format for licensing drivers and ultimately getting them to a road test is important. It not only creates a standard for responsible driving, but also binds people together through their common experiences. Those experiences are routinely communicated to younger generations. Want proof? Most teens and tweens who've never even been behind the wheel of a vehicle can tell you stage by stage what it takes to secure a driver's license. They also know specific stories associated with that journey told to them by their parents and older siblings.

Thus, moving through the system to obtain a driver's license in the US has become a societal rite of passage. And that decipherable system has created a standard of success.

NATURAL KUNG FU: ROUTINELY SUBSTANTIAL

Systematic structure can be a powerfully positive influence in the framework of our daily lives. Wendy Behar, who holds a masters of social work degree (MSW and LMSW) and is an accredited alcohol and substance abuse counselor (CASAC), preaches the benefits of consistency and routines to her clients as a tool to make their lives better and more manageable.

[93]

"The structure of a solid, daily routine can help us to cope with life's ups and downs, as well as fight off anxiety and depression," said Behar, who has been in recovery herself for more than two decades. "Have a general routine about when you'll go to bed each night. Upon waking up in the morning, you should have a checklist of things to do. Breakfast, exercise, and time for self-reflection are extremely important. The mind and body generally go hand in hand. Coping skills are something we all need to develop, and emphasizing structure in our lives can help bring that about."

Is it possible to become too busy and overburdened with routines?

"Not at all. If I want something done, I'll ask a busy person to do it," said Behar. "Busy people understand the concept of time management—something that's absolutely refined through structure. The busiest people tend to be the most productive and successful."

As proof of this concept, in a single day, Wendy meditates, exercises, meets with her clients, writes self-help materials, and keeps in contact with friends, as well as spending quality time with her husband, children, and granddaughter.

"I believe that routines and structure in our daily lives equal productivity," Behar noted. "And that kind satisfaction with ourselves can help to steer us away from negative influences such as drugs and alcohol."

PAUL'S PERSPECTIVE: A HAPPY HOLIDAY

Our family was thrilled to adopt a pup named Galaxy, a black Labrador retriever, as a 2010 holiday present. Dogs can be pretty expensive, and I wasn't really concerned about receiving any other gifts. Sometime prior, my wife, April, had asked me if I wanted anything for myself. I told her that I just needed some new T-shirts and socks.

A "System" of Kung Fu

At the time, I'd been studying Kung Fu with Sifu William for probably eleven months. I was wearing a white shirt to class, which designated me as a beginner—the next two level shirts were green and then red. And I had put an absolute beating on my uniform shirt, with a seam at the collar starting to fray.

On Christmas Eve, April and our daughter, Sabrina, handed me a thin box with a ribbon around it. I shook the box and gave it a listen. I was convinced there was a T-shirt inside.

I was right. Only it wasn't a regular T-shirt. It was a green uniform shirt that read: Moy Yat Kung Fu.

April and Sabrina both had huge smiles on their faces. I didn't want to hurt their feelings but I felt like I just had to tell them, "I can't show up at class wearing a green shirt because I got it for a present. Sifu William has a system. He moves students up when they're ready. Did you buy this online or something?"

My wife took the lead, making a quick apology, saying she didn't know anything about the system of moving students up. But she asked me to try the shirt on anyway, just to see if it would fit.

I put the shirt on and then stood in front of the mirror. It fit and looked great.

That's when the two of them broke out laughing hysterically, and Galaxy even added a bark at the excitement.

"I got that shirt at the school last Saturday when you were at work," my wife said. "I asked Sifu William if I could buy you two new white shirts and he said, 'Let me give you green instead because I'm about to move Paul up.' Then I asked him to keep it a secret until Christmas."

I wore that shirt for the rest of the night, feeling a bit played by my family, but proud as a green-feathered peacock.

Several years later, I was even prouder when Sabrina entered the school and eventually earned a green shirt, too.

Live Life Like a Kung Fu Master

LIFE APPLICATIONS

- You purchase a DIY chair from a furniture outlet . . . only the instructions are in a different language. For a moment, you're annoyed and feeling totally lost. Then you realize that the pictorial diagrams which accompany the words are clear enough for you to begin putting it together.
- As one of many supervisors in a large company, you realize that workers are often confused about whom they should report various day-to-day issues. So you create and publish a flow chart displaying which supervisors handle specific problems.
- Your child is struggling to develop good study habits because they are so overwhelmed by a combination of school, family, organized sports, and social activities. To help them, you sit down together and create a realistic schedule, blocking out specific times during the week for studying and their other activities.
- You'd like to run a marathon next year, but you've never run more than five consecutive miles at once. So you sit down with a friend who has run several marathons to plot out a calendar of gradually increasing your mileage to eventually have the 26.2-mile distance within your grasp.

The secret of getting ahead is getting started.
—Mark Twain

A "System" of Kung Fu

 At the conclusion of chapter two, we viewed a pair of Kung Fu maxims that reflected what we had learned so far. Now that you've progressed in your overall knowledge of the art, here are six more for you to examine and consider. Recognize how the first one in this grouping relates directly back to Sifu William's story in chapter seven about the surprise attack launched against him on a darkened city street.

1. Do not be lax when your opponent is not advancing.
2. Once your opponent moves, his center of gravity changes.
3. Complement the hands with posture to make good use of the center line.
4. The eyes and the mind travel together, paying attention to leading edge of attack.
5. Understand the principles for your training.
6. Protect your own posture.

CHAPTER NINE

Chi Sau and Sticking Energy

*The object of all work is production or accomplishment
and to either of these ends there must be forethought,
system, planning, intelligence, and honest purpose, as
well as perspiration. Seeming to do is not doing.*
—Thomas Edison, inventor

REALISTIC TRAINING IS ABUNDANT in fields such as the military, police, fire, ambulance, medicine, emergency services, sports, entertainment, and many others. It's just a drill until the day it's real. No one knows how you'll react under extreme pressure. But practicing under many of those same potential elements will certainly give you a foothold with which to start.

PHYSICAL ATTRIBUTES

Here is a fairly simplistic description of *chi sau*: it is merely meant to be a guide for the beginner. In actuality, several volumes of

Live Life Like a Kung Fu Master

books could be written on this training exercise, explaining all of its concepts and their subsets in incredible detail.

Often described as the "heart and soul" of Wing Chun Kung Fu, *chi sau* is a training exercise in which two practitioners try to seize control of the center line from one another in order to deliver a strike to a vital area. If the center is won cleanly enough, with control of both the opponent's hands, then a second consecutive strike can be delivered. This follow-up technique is called *fan sau* (returning hand) and normally signals the end of the round.

Despite various techniques being both applied and defended at high speed, *chi sau* is not a fight, nor is it a sparring match. In fact, most of the strikes that land are delivered with far less than substantial power. This is achieved by not extending through the target area with the elbow, negating much of the force produced by the entire body. That's why most practitioners do not use protective gear to participate in *chi sau*.

As a training exercise, *chi sau* can develop great sensitivity in the forward-seeking hands of a practitioner. The pair of players begin by hypothetically sharing the center line, sticking to one another via wrist-to-wrist action. This "sticking energy" is continually applied as the players roll their hands from *tan sau* to *bong sau* and *fuk sau* to *tan sau*.

How vital is the need for sensitivity? Since *chi sau* is played at such close range (remember, wrist to wrist), there isn't enough time to see an incoming strike and then react. You can only feel that you've lost control of the center line, and then rush back to the middle to defend it, hopefully connecting with the incoming strike, which should also be on the center. No matter how it might appear to the casual observer of a *chi sau* round, the players are not chasing the opponent's hands. Rather, they're solely seeking to defend and attack on the center line.

One of the main objectives of *chi sau* is to constantly keep both hands alive, with each operating independently from the other. This goal is combined with maintaining correct body structure, technique position (both the right and left hand), and proper balance—all while working to disrupt the opponent's balance. Hence, *chi sau* can easily be viewed as modern societal standard for multitasking/problem solving. Learning to play correctly will both increase your ability to defend yourself and to negotiate the many simultaneous challenges of life.

> *For a visual demonstration, go to YouTube and search: "Live Life Like a Kung Fu Master—William Moy, Demonstrating Chi Sau."*

FROM MY LIFE: A HOUSE FULL OF STONES

The primary exercise shared between a pair of practitioners in the Wing Chun Kung Fu system is *chi sau*. Traditionally, students view the ability to take part in this exercise as a well-earned reward, usually because it takes a year to a year and a half of diligent training to arrive at that point. Of course, once you've made it to that plateau, you'll look up to discover that the mountain you were so excited to climb has a number of higher peaks. And taking your fledgling *chi sau* skills into a session with a more advanced player can be the equivalent of staring up a sheer facing from a lowly base camp, still miles from where you had hoped to plant your flag. I was no different when I began playing *chi sau*; I had to prepare myself for another major ascent upon the mountain.

Though I would practice at every opportunity, I regularly trained against more experienced classmates who possessed greater skill. One such player was exceptional at exploiting a particular weakness in my hand positioning. As a result, my elbow distanced itself from my body, producing a solid opening for my opponent to strike. This frustrating scenario played out many times over until, during one such session, I called a halt to the proceedings, acknowledging an absolute need for improvement on my part.

During my break, I began intently studying the more accomplished *chi sau* players. I noticed one with even a slighter frame than mine, but his positioning was incredibly flawless, allowing him to protect his center from incoming attacks. Meanwhile, his ability to maintain wrist-to-wrist contact gave him great sensitivity to both feel and create openings in others. Witnessing this served as a powerful example to me that good position, regardless of size and strength, can make all the difference in your Kung Fu.

The concept of occupying space—especially along the center line—not only protects you, but helps to control the actions of your opponent. My father once told me a story that perfectly reflects this idea. Imagine that your house contains something incredibly valuable, perhaps bars of gold. Just outside your door is a band of thieves scheming to break in and steal it all. What would be the best line of defense to thwart them? The answer is to fill your house (physical structure) with rocks, thus occupying all of the space. This will effectively prevent the thieves from even opening the door, let alone entering.

By applying the story's concept to *chi sau*, I was able to maximize my defensive capabilities which, in turn, aided me in creating an offense. The open space along my center line was the house that the thieves, or other players, desired to enter. Not only did I need to better align my skeletal structure to stop them, but an effective defense also required alignment of the three foundational techniques: *tan sau, fuk sau,* and *bong sau.* This combination of improvements essentially jammed the door with rocks, allowing me to operate in an increasingly efficient manner.

And with years of additional dedication and practice, I finally scaled the mountain.

[102]

Chi Sau and Sticking Energy

I learned the value of hard work by working hard.
—Margaret Mead, anthropologist

GLOBAL REFLECTIONS

Among the characteristics of good *chi sau* is the ability to react in the moment, combined with a strong sense of using a single or multiple structures to problem solve. To this end, the zookeepers at the Rio de Janeiro Zoo displayed some amazing Kung Fu during a recent winter heat wave in Brazil that sent the mercury skyrocketing up to 104 degrees. Much of the animal population were so thrown by the unusual weather that they began to shed their winter fur (that would be a wholly different problem later, when the temperatures declined). But what to do in the sweltering moment for the uncomfortable residents?

The quick-thinking zookeepers decided on a temporary change to the structure of the animals' meals, transforming them into cooling ice pops. The fruit-flavored ones—watermelon, pineapple, and grape—for the spider monkeys were hidden amid their habitat to satisfy the creature's need to forage. Of course, fruit wouldn't do for the zoo's predatory animals. So the zookeepers comprised those ice pops of blood and minced meat.

Naturally, you've heard of the film *Kung Fu Panda*. But how about Kung Fu elephants? The Brazilian zookeepers had plenty of faith in their herd. And why not? Elephants possess the largest brain of any land mammal, three times the size of a human. After wrapping large frozen blocks of fruit in their trunks to cool down, the pachyderm crushed the blocks beneath their enormous feet, slurping up the remains.

Baseball catching prospect Dennis Kasumba didn't take the normal route to playing for the Maryland-based Frederick Keys, a summer league filled with players hoping to be drafted by a major league franchise. The orphaned Kasumba was discovered by baseball coach Paul Wafula working in a Ugandan slaughterhouse at the age of fourteen in order to support his grandmother. The coach kindly offered the young man a way out—a replacement job and a spot on a local youth baseball squad. At the time, neither one of them knew the type of Kung Fu Dennis Kasumba would eventually display in chasing his dream to play major-league baseball.

Upon falling in love with the sport, Kasumba understood that he'd need to train relentlessly to compete at the highest levels. But where would the economically depressed youngster find the equipment and training tools he'd need? Well, he simply made them out of the refuse he found on the streets of his hometown, Wakiso.

Fashioning structures to test and improve his athletic ability became second nature to Kasumba. He made makeshift weights out of old tires suspended from both ends of a cement-laden steel bar. Small stacks of bricks became balance beams, as he squatted upon them in a catcher's stance with a heavy iron turn valve tied to his mitt. And a discarded oil drum filled with water served as tool to strengthen his legs as he attempted to jump out of the drum, over and over again, with rubber resistance straps around his shoulders.

The uber-resourceful Kasumba is a model of the *chi sau*/Kung Fu mindset, understanding where your body needs to be and using every tool and structure to get there.

NATURAL KUNG FU: NOTHING SAYS "ZEN" LIKE AN URBAN GARDEN

In *chi sau*, we learn how to control the space in front of us, making it work in our favor and satisfying our own needs. Perhaps the everyday equivalent of such an exercise is mirrored in the work of urban gardeners, who carve out a haven for nature, often within the densest of cityscapes.

Chi Sau and Sticking Energy

A native of Eastern Massachusetts, Christopher Grallert started working on an apple orchard at age twelve. "It was probably a very uncool job for a preteen, picking up fallen apples for ten cents a box. But it actually taught me a lot," recalled Grallert, who is now the president of Green City Growers, an entity focused on bringing sustainable agriculture into the Boston area and its school systems.

"Most people are three to four generations removed from growing their own produce. There's incredible power working in an urban garden space, growing things for consumption within a community. It helps to cure a lack of connecting with the earth. And as a community project, it helps to cure our lack of connecting with one another, remembering how much more alike we are than different. I'm a warrior for that cause," said Grallert, who has over thirty full-time employees working as a tightly knit team in an effort to propagate those outcomes.

Why has gardening become such an important part of Boston Public Schools?

"Students are moved by their own success. They learn patience, and that there's a process to follow for positive results. They get to share that feeling of being successful. We have a curriculum from pre-K through the twelfth grade, including special needs students, which harmonizes with STEM (science, technology, engineering, and mathematics) learning."

Green City Growers' most high-profile space is at Boston's Fenway Park, home of the Boston Red Sox. The garden is adjacent to the stadium's iconic left field wall, dubbed the "Green Monster," which stands nearly forty feet high, resting 310 feet from home plate.

"The garden is above the administrative offices of the Red Sox. The team's ownership believes strongly in sustainability and community. And there is probably no better place to exhibit what's possible in a hyper-urban setting than having a three-thousand-square-foot garden producing organic vegetables in that space, which is one of the biggest tourist attractions in Boston. There are usually gasps of excitement and awe whenever visitors first see it."

Ultimately, Grallert hopes that urban gardens bring as much positivity to the daily lives of Bostonians as it has brought to his own life.

"Magic happens in gardens," emphasized Grallert. "Gardening inspires energy and enthusiasm. Personally, it has always helped to focus my energies, bringing me to a place of balance."

PAUL'S PERSPECTIVE: THE RIDE ALONG

For several decades, Alex Miteff drove limos, livery cabs, and vans, hauling passengers all over the five boroughs of New York City. Every time I got a chance to ride along with Alex, it was like getting a history lesson. I mostly rode with Alex and a dozen other passengers to the racetrack where I was working as a sportswriter. You see the Argentine-born Miteff, who stood 6-foot-1 and weighed well over two hundred pounds, had a previous career as a prize-fighter.

Right over his rearview mirror, Alex had taped up a photo of himself in a pair of trunks and boxing gloves. The athlete in the photo was a lot younger and probably thirty pounds lighter, but you could clearly tell that it was Alex, who had won the gold medal in the 1955 Pan Am Games, held in Mexico City, as a heavyweight.

Of course, the story that everyone wanted to hear was about when Alex fought a young Cassius Clay (soon to embrace the Muslim faith and become Muhammad Ali) at Freedom Hall in Louisville, Kentucky, on October 7, 1961.

It was an undefeated Clay's ninth professional bout, after winning the gold medal in the 1960 Olympics in Rome as a light heavyweight.

How did Alex do in the ring against Clay?

Chi Sau and Sticking Energy

"It was an even fight for a while. I landed a good shot or two and got my respect from him. But mostly, he carried me as far as he wanted me to go and then put me away," Miteff once told us while driving his van on the streets of Queens. "I lost to the greatest fighter of all time. He kept tying up my right hand, and that took away a lot of my power."

Alex was stopped by a technical knockout (TKO) in the sixth round.

During the post-fight interviews, Clay's trainer, the Hall of Famer Angelo Dundee, talked about how he had taught his fighter to "stick" to the opponent's right hand, and how when he eventually learned to stick to the left hand as well, his fighter might become unbeatable.

Sticking? I often wondered if Ali had mastered the boxing version of Kung Fu's *chi sau*, gaining control of an opponent's limbs and significantly defusing their power by disrupting momentum—you can actually see the fight against Alex on YouTube!

Was Alex unlucky enough to run up against this emerging technique, implemented by a seemingly other-worldly-talented pugilist?

More than a decade later, in a heavyweight championship fight in Zaire (now the Democratic Republic of the Congo), billed as "The Rumble in the Jungle," Ali used that perfected sticking action on both hands to control the immense power of George Foreman to slow and weigh down his arm, even while Ali executed his famed rope-a-dope tactic, in which Foreman punched himself into exhaustion.

Alex and Muhammad Ali struck up a friendship over the years. They both appeared in the film *Requiem for a Heavyweight* (1962) alongside Anthony Quinn, Jackie Gleason, Mickey Rooney, and Julie Harris. Whenever Ali visited NYC, Alex would show up at his Manhattan hotel to reminisce and pose for pictures with "The Champ."

Despite all of the time that has passed since I've ridden with Alex, I can still close my eyes, feel the bumps in the road—riding in that badly-in-need-of-new-shock-absorbers van—and hear his gravelly voice telling those magnificent tales.

Coauthor Paul Volponi playing chi sau with his daughter, Sabrina, in the Colosseum in Rome.

LIFE APPLICATIONS

- You're traveling at 60 mph in the right lane of a two-lane highway. A vehicle that is several car lengths ahead of you stops abruptly. The left lane beside you is occupied, and you've already noticed that the car directly behind you is traveling closer to you than you'd like. With little option left to avoid an accident, you immediately steer onto the shoulder, even though you don't have a totally clear vision of what's in the foreground there.
- Your child has built their first kite and can't wait to fly it. Unfortunately, there's currently little to no wind at the local park. So you make the decision to drive the extra twenty-five minutes to the beach where the differences

in air pressure above the sandy beach and ocean waters make winds much more likely.
- The wooden toolshed in your backyard is beginning to lean toward one side. So you straighten it with a wedge, allowing you to correctly add more permanent means of support to the structure.
- In learning to juggle, you realize that your focus needs to be divided among multiple simultaneous events, while your right and left hand work both in concert and independently from one another.

Being a fish out of water is tough. But that's how you evolve.

—Kumail Nanjiani, Pakistani-American actor and comedian

SIGHT UNSEEN

The legend of the blind Kung Fu master has piqued the curiosity of both Hollywood studios and audiences worldwide for generations. The most recent incarnation of this character comes in the *Star Wars* franchise as actor and martial artist Donnie Yen, who played the title role of Ip Man in the four-film saga, assumed the part of Chirrut Îmwe, a blind, Kung Fu–like swordsman, in *Rogue One*. Moviegoers cheered the character's every move as he fought on feeling and anticipation, rather than sight.

Marvel Comics's Daredevil character, aka Matt Murdock, is also a blind martial artist whose other senses have heighted to a level where being blind is no longer a handicap for him. Daredevil made his debut back in 1964 and was the brainchild of famed writer Stan Lee and artist Bill Everett.

(continued next page)

Live Life Like a Kung Fu Master

In 1972, ABC-TV released an action-western series entitled *Kung Fu*. The series starred actor David Carradine (who future generations would recognize as Bill from director Quentin Tarantino's martial arts–inspired *Kill Bill* series of films) as Kwai Chang Caine, a Shaolin monk forced to seek exile in the western territories of the US. One of Caine's primary teachers at the Shaolin Temple was master Po (actor Keye Luke), a blind Kung Fu master who excelled with a staff that also doubled as a walking stick for the aged character.

Is there any reality to Hollywood's portrayal of the blind martial artist?

Yes. In fact, there are many blind martial artists in the world today. They are training, thriving, and gaining great personal advantages in their daily lives from the arts, including increased spatial awareness. Those at the highest levels are competing at judo in the Paralympics, with taekwondo possibly ready to soon field visually impaired competitors as well. There are also many sightless wrestlers relying on the feel of grappling to give them all of the information needed to execute moves and win, even against sighted opponents.

How about Kung Fu and the training exercise of *chi sau*?

Some practitioners have put on public demonstrations of playing *chi sau* while blindfolded. You can find videos of this activity fairly easily on YouTube. Since *chi sau* is so reliant on a practitioner's sensitivity, and the exercise is conducted at close range where timing and control of the center line are more vital than seeing an incoming attack, visually impaired players can be incredibly successful at it.

CHAPTER TEN

RELAXATION OVER TENSENESS

A crust eaten in peace is better than a banquet partaken in anxiety.

—Aesop

RELAXATION IS THE KEY to preforming better. Injecting it into almost any endeavor will serve you far greater than the false notion that a certain amount of tenseness equals more focus.

PHYSICAL ATTRIBUTES

Learning to relax both your body and mind is a huge part of successfully incorporating Kung Fu into your life. If someone were to physically attack you on the street, trying to take you off balance and move you from Point A to Point B, being stiff and tense would put you at a supreme disadvantage. When you are tense you become more rigid, providing your attacker with a virtual handle on your body in much the same way that you might easily grasp a teapot by the handle to pour out its contents. Simple and straightforward. Your rigid arm or shoulder will serve your attacker in that regard. But when you are relaxed, your body is better able to absorb force, moving with it to a degree in order to redirect it.

For example, take your right hand and grab your left wrist tightly, until you are almost cutting off the circulation. Your right hand, now extremely tense, is actually frozen there, unable to do anything else. What's the only way to enable the release the left wrist and move onto a different objective? The right hand must first relax! That's one reason we use a *fuk sau* in place of a grab. It allows the hand to stay relaxed by using the power of a sinking elbow.

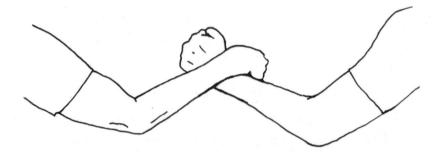

Part of becoming more relaxed is achieved through diligent training. You've already been introduced to Wing Chun Kung Fu's first form, *Siu Nim Tao*, which, if performed daily, should be a huge ally to you in achieving calmness, even in the midst of battle. Another important part of maintaining relaxation is trust. In a fight, you must have trust in your Kung Fu skills. You must trust that your training has put you in the right position, securing proper distance. You must trust that you can stop an incoming strike by using *pak da* (if circumstances dictate that is the correct technique), and thus immediately put pressure back on your opponent with the near simultaneous block and punch. Because the truth is that you won't have time to think; there will only be

Relaxation Over Tenseness

enough time for an instinctive reaction. If you're thinking about your possible response, it's already too late.

Naturally, this trust in your training will carry over into your everyday activities. You'll certainly face career, school, family, and social challenges significantly more than you will be thrust into bodily combat (we can only hope). Once again, Kung Fu translates as *time + effort = skill*. So if you've put in the time to properly prepare yourself for such challenges, then calmness—along with intense focus—should prevail.

FROM MY LIFE: A VOLUNTEER FROM THE AUDIENCE

I was attending a Kung Fu conference where I was scheduled to be one of the many speakers. It was my plan to give a talk and demonstration on *chi sau*, something that normally excites and pleases the attendees with so many practitioners focused on improving their abilities concerning that exercise. In the past, I had given many such lectures accompanied by physical demonstrations, so I was quite relaxed in the moments leading up to my time on stage. In fact, I was looking forward to connecting with the crowd, sharing my knowledge with them, as well as hearing their questions and reactions in return.

The only thing different about this particular demo was going to be that my usual *chi sau* partner during such presentations wasn't in attendance on that day. Nevertheless, I felt well prepared and confident as the host announced my name and I stepped onto the stage.

My lecture started off well, and I felt that the crowd was receptive and interested. When it came time for me to give a visual example on the concepts about which I had spoken, I asked for a volunteer from the audience.

A hand in the front row immediately shot up. The gentleman appeared quite eager to lend a hand, or two hands as it were (*chi sau* humor). Plus, I already knew him as a kind and caring individual who possessed good Kung Fu in life and was serious about the art.

As we touched hands to begin the demonstration, I quickly felt the tenseness in his body, which was probably due to working in public with a sifu, and the many sets of eyes focused upon us. I rolled with him through a few positions, making my hands as light and relaxed as possible, hoping it would ease his tension. Only that did not affect a change.

I went forward with the demonstration anyway, neither desiring to disappoint the crowd nor embarrass him by changing partners. As I tried to maneuver our hands into the proper position to illustrate a point that I had made in my lecture, our timing wasn't there due to his tenseness.

I quickly ended the demo on a short note, and the disappointment in the crowd and my partner was palpable—not to mention the disappointment in myself. Today, as I look back on that moment, I wish that *I* had been more at ease concerning our *chi sau*. I could have explained the situation to the audience and my partner, or changed partners. I could have even changed the demonstration from a *chi sau* setting to a real-life attack, highlighting the same principle.

It's a solid reminder that there are times when even sifus aren't relaxed enough.

> *Neither comprehension nor learning can take place in an atmosphere of anxiety.*
> —Rose Kennedy, Kennedy Family matriarch

SALES FORCE/CENTER STAGE/CLANK!

There's a new product on your showroom floor—an ultra-deluxe massage chair with all the bells and whistles, including Italian

Relaxation Over Tenseness

leather upholstery, several different intensity settings, heat, and an option to recline. It's advertised as "The Greatest Massage Chair on the Market." It's a tag line your company wants all of its salesforce to talk up at every opportunity. As a supervisor, it's your job to make sure that happens. But you already know that several of your best salespeople won't recommend any product to a customer unless they thoroughly believe in its claims. So a week before the high-priced chair is to debut in your store, you personally unpack three of them and set them up in the employee lounge. This way, your salespeople can decide for themselves whether or not they would be comfortable trumpeting the manufacture's claims.

Perhaps your youngest child has a handful of lines in the school play and is showing signs of anxiety about having to speak on stage. You decide the best way to ease that tension is to provide a series of makeshift audiences in the weeks leading up to the performance. Every night at dinner, the entire family puts their meal on hold while sitting around the table as your youngest stands up to recite their lines, followed by a round of applause. You also arrange for several neighbors to drop in and participate. And when your youngest is alone practicing in their room, you have them line up their stuffed animals to observe. It's all in a combined effort to lessen anxiety through repeated exposure to a suitable substitute for being on stage.

Imagine that it's an intersquad scrimmage of a high school basketball team in their own gym. The coach has a pair of refs on the floor and the time clock running to simulate the conditions of a real game. With just two seconds left in the faux contest with the score tied, one of the players is fouled and goes to the line for a pair of free throws. Their first attempt is short and flat, hitting the rim with an off-key *clank*. The player, visibly upset at the miss, is still standing at the foul line with their feet in the exact same position, waiting for the ref to deliver the ball to them for their second free throw. From the bench the coach jumps up and calls to the shooter, "Keep off the line and walk a few steps. Then reset yourself." The prudent advice is aimed at both easing tension in the player and setting a new structure in place of the one that has just failed.

NATURAL KUNG FU: CHANGING MODES

Over the past two decades, if you're a sports fan, you've almost certainly seen the work of TV camera operator Chris Fiala. And if you didn't realize that he was even there, all the better.

"My job is to be totally relaxed and smooth in moving the camera to follow the live action. The audience should never see their picture jut, or even think that there is a camera operator. That small jut on the screen is a sign of tenseness in the operator's movements," said Fiala, a Kung Fu practitioner and amateur ice hockey player. "To shoot properly, I often have to shift my feet while turning the wide angle of the camera nearly 180 degrees. That calls for relaxation in my hands and steps."

Displaying that kind of relaxation behind a camera isn't always easy. One of Fiala's first assignments was to shoot in the exasperating winds of a nor'easter. Another time, he sat alone in a fifty-foot-high tower in the face of heavy rain and lightning, with the expectation that he would be just as smooth with his movements as if he were shooting under normal conditions.

Chris Fiala grew up a huge fan of Bruce Lee and studied "hard" martial arts as a youngster, where overpowering an obstacle was the primary mindset. When Chris first walked into Sifu William Moy's school as a fledgling student, he had no idea that his hero, Bruce Lee, was part of the lineage, and would now be considered his Kung Fu uncle.

"That alone was some solid motivation for me to learn Kung Fu," recalled Fiala, who stands an imposing 6-foot-1 and a half, weighing 225 pounds.

In some of his earliest exercises, Fiala tried to lean on his size and strength. However, several much smaller and older students were able to exploit his tenseness to place him in compromising positions.

"Don't try harder. Try easier," was the response from his more experienced classmates. This approach didn't come automatically to an individual as big and strong as Fiala.

"Over time, as I learned more about the art adjusting my thinking and physical responses to become more relaxed," said Fiala, who found that this also helped him as a hockey player. "In Kung Fu, you can feel your opponent's movements when your limbs are touching one another's. I was able to carry that sensitivity over to the ice as well. Now, whenever I tangle up with another player against the boards, I feel like I can anticipate their next move, and even feel the puck better on my stick."

PAUL'S PERSPECTIVE: MY ADOPTED SON

After six years of teaching incarcerated teens on Rikers Island, I picked up a new assignment from the New York City Department of Education: working with teens in a Brooklyn-based day drug treatment center.

A few months into the job, I received a new student named Carlos, who took his place among the fifteen or so other teens in the treatment center's one-room schoolhouse. Carlos was having a tough time adjusting to his new educational surroundings, and probably even the tougher task of removing illegal drugs from his life. He'd been in several tense arguments with other students over absolutely nothing in just a short period of time. I recall having a real talk with him about resolving conflicts in a more relaxed way.

One morning, Carlos and I exited the same subway car of a G train, and started walking the handful of blocks to the treatment center together. In an instant, we were confronted by a wall of seven teens blocking the sidewalk, four boys and three girls. They refused to let us pass, barking at Carlos about some trouble he'd started on the street the day before.

They were talking tough, but I sensed they didn't really want to fight or we'd have been in an all-out brawl already. So I stepped directly in front of Carlos, introducing myself as his teacher and him as "my adopted son."

"When I get him to school, I'm going to see that he's punished for acting stupid with you guys," I announced. That could have been Carlos's opportunity to take off running. I would have thrown an innocent block on the first one to chase after him, giving Carlos another twenty-five-yard advantage. But when I glanced back behind me, the normally tough-talking Carlos appeared frozen with fear. So it was up to me to keep that posse relaxed and talk our way out of it.

Just then, a traffic enforcement officer came down the block, checking inspection stickers on a row of parked cars.

"Hey, officer, "where's the nearest high school from here?" I called to her.

"That would be Brooklyn Tech, a couple of blocks over," she answered.

I turned to our temporary captors, all of whom were in possession of book bags, and said, "Please, don't make me come over there on my period off and point you out to security and the deans."

Maybe it was the word "please," but that statement of mine, coupled with an additional promise to punish Carlos, finally got that wall of teens to begrudgingly part for us.

Carlos remained silent until we reach the treatment center, before he simply said, "See you in class, Teach." But later that morning, I did overhear him retell the story to the other students in our school. Only his colorful version had him a bit more in command of the situation.

Relaxation Over Tenseness

I'd like to be able to tell you how that incident changed Carlos's attitude. That he became a dedicated student and kicked his drug habit. But things like that mostly happen in the movies, close to the conclusion. Luckily for Carlos, though, his life was still in its opening acts.

LIFE APPLICATIONS

- You feel yourself getting tense about an upcoming meeting with your boss. To combat this feeling, you make a list of ten reasons detailing your value as an employee. Just prior to the meeting, you read the list to yourself.
- Several times a month you wake in the middle of the night feeling incredibly anxious for no discernable reason. So you learn some brief meditation exercises and even use a recording of tranquil forest sounds to help you relax during those moments and fall back asleep.
- You hear your child crying in the middle of the night. You hurriedly get out of bed and in the darkness stub your toe on a piece of furniture. You'd like to scream out in both pain and frustration, but you realize that you need to stay calm to better respond to your child's cries.
- The fire alarm sounds in a large building, and you can actually smell smoke. As you're exiting your fifth-floor office you see someone frantically pushing the elevator button. That's when you calmly escort them over to the staircase, talking to them in an even-toned voice every step of the way.

I've learned over the years that if you start thinking about the race, it stresses you out a little bit. I just try to relax and think about video games, what I'm going do after the race, what I'm going to do just to chill.

—Usain Bolt, Olympic champion sprinter

Live Life Like a Kung Fu Master

HONORED GUEST: TAK WAH ENG (CHINATOWN, NYC/HONG KONG)

Truly embodying the humble spirit of Kung Fu is Grandmaster Tak Wah Eng, a renowned teacher and martial artist who has been honing his craft for more than four decades in New York City's Chinatown. "I never tell people that I do Kung Fu. I want them to see me as an individual, to get to know me as Tak. I never try to sell them on the art, even though I live it as an example," said Master Eng, who studied as a teenager under the tutelage of Grandmaster Wai Hong. "Kung Fu is an art about culture, philosophy and tradition. I don't like to see it commercialized in any way."

In 1967, Eng, along with his family, immigrated to New York City from Hong Kong at the age of seventeen. "Despite the passing of time, some things remain the same and rarely change. There will always be bullies. Young people come to Kung Fu to learn how to stand up for themselves, to learn how to fight back and toughen themselves. They learn the art and gain confidence. They begin to understand that you don't have to be afraid. That you can protect yourself. Only when threatened should you use your Kung Fu skills to fight," emphasized Master Eng.

Expressing himself through various mediums has always been a passionate aspect of Master Eng's life. For many years, he trained and worked as a graphic artist for an advertising agency, with his work appearing in dozens of national ad campaigns and TV commercials.

"I'm grateful to be able to express my energy onto a canvas. My art has become much more personal over the years, using different brushstrokes to emphasize colors. In a sense, it's the way I feel and move while I'm performing Kung Fu, only it's captured in a work of art."

(continued next page)

Relaxation Over Tenseness

You might also know Master Eng's work from the fight scenes he helped to choreograph in the action/martial arts film *Romeo Must Die* (2000), starring Jet Li and singer/actress Aaliyah.

"I learned a lot from the stunt people and the director. You need to understand about camera angles, what will look good on film and what won't—how to make movie magic. Working with Jet Li, showing him a Northern style of Kung Fu, and Aaliyah, who is originally from New York City, was wonderful. I thought it was a really good action movie."

How does Master Eng see Kung Fu helping his students' daily lives?

"It's about having balance in your life, and not going too far to one extreme or another. It ties in with breathing and meditation. Learn how to use your breathing, and how to borrow energy and power from the ground, the earth beneath you."

Eng has witnessed the process of his own Kung Fu changing over these many years of performing, teaching, and studying the art. "My knowledge has increased, and I'm learning even more. I guess I'm no longer a *beginner*," said Master Eng, in a wry tone. "The art is so deep, and I'm open to many ideas. But through the years, I've come to learn that 'soft' energy is the best. I play a lot of forms that way now. I remember meeting Moy Yat long ago. He was always a gentleman to me and a friend of my teacher. Moy Yat used to say, 'You don't need a hammer to hit someone,' referring to 'hard' energy. 'You just need to perfect your technique.' He was right. Nowadays, I use more soft energy in my Kung Fu."

CHAPTER ELEVEN

Redirecting External Forces

There is no rejection, there is only redirection.
—Matt Haig, author and journalist

WHEN YOU CAN TAKE the negativity aimed at you, be it words or actions, and send it somewhere else to reside, then you've really accomplished something to enhance your daily life.

PHYSICAL ATTRIBUTES

It's true that Kung Fu practitioners can deliver some incredibly powerful strikes, including some from just a few inches away. That's reminiscent of many "hard" martial arts such as Karate and Taekwondo, which emphasize the idea of force vs. force. But like the diametrically opposed blended concepts that constitute the Chinese theory of Yin and Yang (discussed in more depth at the conclusion of chapter seventeen), Kung Fu makes use of a "soft" side as well. One of the ways this materializes is in our use of redirecting external forces, instead of trying to meet them head-on with a superior show of brute strength.

How can we redirect external forces? The proper use of angles helps us to diffuse force, greatly lessening its impact and putting us in superior position to respond through an attack of our own. This can be seen in our use of *pak sau* and *pak da*, in which the palm doesn't intercept the front of the incoming fist. Instead, both of those techniques confront the attack from the side, normally just above the wrist. *Lop sau* also uses a side-angled approach in grabbing the opponent's incoming strike before sending its energy downward and away from our body. The proper use of a *bong sau* to address a strike is dependent on a side angle, too, incorporating a shift in the defender's weight to the leg supporting the technique to further absorb and disperse the force.

> *For a visual demonstration, go to YouTube and search: "Live Life Like a Kung Fu Master—William Moy, Demonstrating Redirecting Techniques."*

As my father used to say, "Kung Fu gets into your bones." And once you're introduced to these physical applications, I'm confident that you'll be using their social equivalent in your everyday dealings with others. Whether that's choosing the correct angle to begin a difficult conversation or lessening potential conflict by softening your initial response to those who may be inclined to escalate matters in which they don't get their way. Remember, the idea of firmly standing your ground often includes giving way just enough to secure your best position.

Redirecting External Forces

FROM MY LIFE: THE LONG COMMUTE

I once had an early morning side job transporting senior citizens to an adult daycare from their homes in Queens, New York. I enjoyed it for the most part, and found it to be gratifying work. Without someone to drive them to the center, most of the seniors whom I transported daily (because they were either unable to drive themselves or take mass transportation) would have been homebound for much of the day, especially during the winter months. By spending their days at the center, they received a hot breakfast and lunch, socialization, and could partake in various activities to invigorate their minds and bodies. Caring for seniors, referred to as filial piety, is an important part of my Asian culture. With my own grandparents having long passed away, I saw this as way of giving back to those who came before me. And with two growing sons to support, an extra weekly paycheck was of great help to my wife and me.

This might have been a noble job in theory. But the reality of driving a twelve-passanger van during rush hour, often filled with very opinionated seniors, offered some incredibly testing moments.

It was my third day on the job. Traffic was at a near standstill, and I had a new passenger to pick up in a nearly filled van. Despite being very familiar with the roads and neighborhoods in Queens, I couldn't immediately find the new address.

One of my passengers, who apparently didn't possess an internal filter between his brain and mouth, began hammering me verbally.

"We've been down this block before. Can't you read numbers? I don't care if this driver's new, we're already twenty minutes late."

Then my tormentor actually found an ally in the van, adding a second voice to the barrage of negative comments. In all honesty, it was really beginning to annoy me. I even had a fleeting vision of leaving them both by the side of the road.

And some of the other passengers, who'd been giving me a look of sympathy, probably would have supported such a move.

After picking up the last passenger, I estimated that we were still thirty minutes from the senior center. That's when I mentally called my Kung Fu into play. I needed a way to redirect these negative external forces away from me and into something positive. So I began to intensely focus on my driving, cheering myself on with every lane change to beat a light about to turn red. One of the passengers even praised a deft move I made around a stalled vehicle.

In embracing the act of driving, making that my main goal, I avoided any weight given to that pair's criticisms, even if just in my own mind.

We arrived at our destination fourteen minutes to the good of my estimate, and not a minute too soon as far as I was concerned.

Before I headed home, my supervisor called me into her office.

"I heard from some of our clients that you had a challenging morning."

I replied with an understated, "Yes."

"Just remember, William, seniors often become kids again when they get frustrated."

Nodding my head, I left the conversation at that.

But, in my mind, I wish I'd had the power, just for a little while, to send those two senior-adolescents to a well-deserved time out.

The dogma of science is that the will cannot possibly affect external forces, and I think that's just ridiculous.
—William S. Burroughs, writer and visual artist

NOT SO SOUR NOTES/E-3

Early in 1966, Bob Dylan was one of the hottest musicians on the planet. Fans clamored to hear his acoustic folk songs such as

Redirecting External Forces

"Blowin' in the Wind" and "Mr. Tambourine Man," as he filled venues across the country. But in February of that year, Dylan changed his style and went electric, embarking on a world tour with a rock and roll band (named The Band) backing him up. The reaction was not what Dylan had expected. His loyal fans hated the new music and booed him unmercifully, only applauding one or two of the older songs done in his original folky style.

But Dylan wouldn't relent. He and The Band eventually began to redirect the negative outcry by pulling tightly together in an us-against-the-world mentality. More than a half a century later, that music, which received so much criticism at the time, is now considered to be among Dylan's best work.

Defined by an error? Late in Game Six of the 1986 World Series between the New York Mets and Boston Red Sox, batter Mookie Wilson of the Mets hit a slow roller to first baseman Bill Buckner. The baseball somehow bounced between Buckner's legs (an E-3 in baseball parlance), opening the door for the Mets to win Game Six, along with Game Seven two nights later to virtually snatch the World Series away from the Sox, who hadn't won a championship since 1918.

Boston fans ridiculed Buckner, a former batting champion and All-Star, making him the scapegoat for the team's collapse. It got so bad that the Red Sox franchise felt compelled to release Buckner midway through the following season.

Buckner was acutely aware of the criticism and the ugly remarks fans would shout at him on the field. The player had only two choices: redirect what he'd heard or hang up his spikes and call it a career. To Buckner's credit, his intense focus, especially as a hitter, got him through the worst of it as he played for another three seasons, despite dealing with debilitating leg injuries.

Much to everyone's surprise, the Red Sox re-signed Bill Buckner in 1990. He even received a standing ovation from the home crowd at Fenway Park on Opening Day, proving that his

Live Life Like a Kung Fu Master

ability to pull through a tough situation obviously impressed many of the same fans who previously booed him.

NATURAL KUNG FU: Y AND X

Researcher Stacey Korolkova started studying Wing Chun Kung Fu with Sifu William as a teenager in high school. "I got into the art for reasons of self-defense," recalled Stacey. "I wanted to learn how to better protect myself."

Korolkova, who is currently among a roster of laboratory researchers diligently working to discover a cure to defeat HIV, had an immediate affinity for the art, with her older Kung Fu brothers (*si hings*) impressed by her attention to detail and toughness. But there was another attribute that set Stacey apart from most of her classmates: she was a female, one of only two attending the Chinatown branch of Moy's' school at the time.

"A female friend of mine who'd been training there had told me about the school, and I decided to join," said Korolkova. "It really didn't matter to me that all of the other students were guys because, in my mind, I was thinking that I'd just train with my friend."

But some unexpected external forces came into play. And Stacey's friend, who suddenly found herself pregnant, stopped coming to class, leaving Stacey as the school's lone female student. Her plan of only training with another female needed redirection.

"When I progressed to a point where I'd throw and receive strikes, Sifu suggested that I get a chest guard."

Stacey wasn't pleased with the idea. No one else was wearing one, and she didn't want to stand out as different from her classmates.

"First, I showed up with a guard that could be worn under my shirt. But Sifu insisted that I wear one on the outside. The idea was to make the other students feel comfortable about hitting me in the chest, as much as it was about protecting me."

Redirecting External Forces

A few years into her study, Stacey believed that she had reached her goal and was ready to move on to other pursuits. "I met with Sifu and told him that I already knew how to punch and kick. Only he had this look on his face like there was a lot more that I needed to learn. So I stayed."

Over her subsequent years at the school, Stacey helped to usher in more than a dozen new female students, including her two younger sisters. She also credits studying Kung Fu with helping to develop the courage and focus to follow her heart academically.

"I remember trying to decide on a major in college. I actually met with Sifu to discuss it, and he was of great help to me. I was interested in international relations, but my parents were pushing me to study math. He didn't try to tell me what to do. Instead, he let me know that he had the confidence in me that I'd become my own person."

LIFE APPLICATIONS

- You've served what you believe is the winning ace in a tennis match. But your opponent has called your serve "out by an inch." You're convinced that it was in and you argue the point, but your opponent sticks to their original call. Will you succumb to these external forces testing you? Will anger undermine your focus and cause you to serve the next ball into the net? Or will you divert these forces through internal focus and succeed at serving another ace?

- It's Sunday night and you have just brainstormed several new ideas that you'd like to share with your colleagues that could ease the burden of the upcoming workweek. Only your company's internet platform is down for repairs. So you sketch your ideas out on paper, make a dozen copies,

and have them waiting in your coworkers' physical boxes early Monday morning.
- Scary movies just aren't your thing and tend to make you jumpy. To get some control over your reactions, try watching such a film at home with the volume muted, removing the screams and tense music.
- Someone tries to pull you toward them against your will. Instead of fighting the force by pulling away, you use their own energy against them by quickly coming forward into their space and disturbing their balance.

A republic of this kind, able to withstand an external force, may support itself without any internal corruptions.
—Alexander Hamilton, statesman and one of the founding fathers of the United States of America

SETTING YOUR SAILS FOR SUCCESS
Both Kung Fu practitioners and sailors can be absolute experts at redirecting external forces. We've examined how a martial artist might go about it. So now let's look at a sailor's skill set. In their case, it's the powerful force of the wind that they've learned to redirect.

It's easy for us to visualize a sailboat being pushed by the wind, especially when that boat and the wind are heading in the same direction. But what happens when the wind is blowing in the opposite direction of a sailor's intended destination?

Think of a sailboat as an airplane on its side, with the sail being a wing raised vertically. Sailors will choose an angle at which to set their sails, so that the opposing wind is blowing on both the inside, stretching it taut, and outside of the sail. The camber or teardrop

(continued next page)

[130]

Redirecting External Forces

shape that is made, just like the wing of an airplane, causes the wind to travel faster on the outside of the sail (because it's a longer distance) than the inside. This increase in speed causes a decrease in pressure, creating lift. Only this form of lift doesn't bring the boat up (remember the boat's wing is vertical, not horizontal). Instead, the lift from the sail propels the boat at an angle, sort of sideways.

You may be thinking to yourself, *Then why does the sailboat go forward, and not at the angle the sail is catching the wind?*

Well, there's another wing you can't readily see. It's the camber-shaped keel beneath the sailboat, with the water both pushing and pulling on it, also creating lift. But in the exact opposite direction of the sail. The two opposing forces balance each other out and the sailboat goes straight, even without the wind at its back.

Now that's some nautical Kung Fu!

CHAPTER TWELVE

FACING AND HELPING HANDS

You should never view your challenges as a disadvantage. Instead, it's important for you to understand that your experience facing and overcoming adversity is actually one of your biggest advantages.
—Michelle Obama, Former First Lady

NEVER LOSE SIGHT OF what's directly in front of you, no matter what the challenge may be. Keep that challenge focused in your center, and never turn your vision away from it. If you can do this, you'll see plenty of options and multiple paths to help achieve your ultimate goal.

PHYSICAL ATTRIBUTES

In Wing Chun Kung Fu, the concept of maintaining correct facing with an opponent is called *doi ying*, which translates as *facing the shape*. The shape, in this context, is the human form posing a potential threat to us either during an actual physical

[133]

Live Life Like a Kung Fu Master

confrontation or in the moments prior, when your Kung Fu has alerted you to a possible unfolding situation that could escalate.

Our goal is to face this "shape," with our center line aligned to its center, if that shape is directly facing us. If it is not—for example, it may be in a side stance perpendicular to the direction in which we're facing—we must focus to keep our center line aligned with the center of the mass that is in our direct line of sight.

Why are we so absorbed with keeping the correct facing, in staying *doi ying*? Well, it grants us superior position, allowing for the equal usage of all four of our limbs to address a threat without having to reposition ourselves.

Consider this point: Assume a side stance with either your right or left shoulder facing the center line of an imaginary opponent. Now stretch your lead arm out forward. Then stretch your trailing arm forward. The two arms do not have equal length in a side stance, with the trailing arm being considerably shorter to the target. The two cannot become equal again without you taking the time to shift your hips.

But when you take the correct facing, with your center line *doi ying* to the target, both arms are of equal length. Why is that critical? You've already learned the basics of techniques such as of *pak da* and *lop da*, in which one hand is vital in helping the other to succeed. These are called "helping hands," and are specific to the Wing Chun system.

Naturally, if the opponent moves (changes direction or angle), then we must move to keep our facing. When we lose facing it is referred to as being *sut ying*. Failure to stay *doi ying* sacrifices our superior position, severely handicapping our ability to use helping hands and leaving both our side and back vulnerable to attack.

Facing and Helping Hands

For a visual demonstration, go to YouTube and search: "Live Life Like a Kung Fu Master—William Moy, Demonstrating Good Facing/Helping Hands."

FROM MY LIFE: HOME IS WHERE THE KUNG FU IS

In my earliest days of training Kung Fu, keeping my facing and staying *doi ying* with my partner during *chi sau* drills was incredibly frustrating. Since I was still struggling to acquire some of the foundational qualities we've discussed in prior chapters—structure and positioning, maintaining the proper distance, remaining relaxed, and sticking via wrist-to-wrist energy—I became extremely vulnerable to being maneuvered. I suppose my biggest challenge was continually applying the proper angle because, whenever I didn't, practitioners with more skill left me facing an invisible opponent while I was still directly on the center line.

Just imagine playing a game of Marco Polo in a swimming pool on a summer's day. I'd say "Marco," and every reply of "Polo" would continually be coming from somewhere behind me. Not a good scenario for success.

But, over time, as my Kung Fu started to develop and take shape, I remembered my constant loss of good facing and why it had happened. It was a lesson I took with me through life and learned to project onto other things.

In college, I made sure that I had the relevant class notes and required texts on the reading lists before I sat down to study for an exam. Whenever I had a new job, I focused on knowing the responsibilities and what was expected of someone holding my position.

So my early struggles with being *doi ying* actually helped me in many future endeavors.

Perhaps that facing lesson was never more valuable to me than when my wife and I purchased an older house that needed a lot of repairs. We were each working full-time, and at the time

[135]

had a one-year-old child. So every borrowed hour put into renovations needed to be spent efficiently. My hard and fast rule was not to begin a specific fix unless I understood exactly how it was done, what the common beginner mistakes might be, as well as having the correct tools and materials on hand. I also had help from some of my students and extended Kung Fu family members who understood construction. Together, we painted, plastered, put up new sheetrock, replaced windows, and rehung doors.

The most gratifying part, besides the end result of having the type of home in which my wife and I had always dreamed of raising a family, was that all the hard work was done correctly the first time. That saved us precious hours and made the renovations more economical.

I humbly have my Kung Fu background and learning experiences in the art to thank for that.

> *We learn martial arts as helping weakness. You never fight*
> *for people to get hurt. You're always helping people.*
> —Jackie Chan

PROFESSIONAL/FAMILY

Imagine that you are suddenly transferred into a different department at your job. You would be unfamiliar with your new coworkers and their system of pulling together as a team. Should you be watching them for clues? Will you be given an official introduction by a supervisor? In reality, it may be several weeks until you have absorbed all the details of your new surroundings and are able to get back to the standard of productivity you expect from yourself. Can you be malleable enough to fit into a new way of doing things? Can you incorporate your best ideas and practices from your former department into this one? The truth is that

Facing and Helping Hands

you'll have to be observant, studying the entire picture before the answers begin to take shape.

Perhaps your sister and brother-in-law are forced to move in with your family for several weeks. Yes, you've spent time at each other's homes before, but you've never lived together as adults. Will you sit down for a face-to-face talk, discussing household rules and responsibilities?

What you will most likely come to realize is that after two days of misunderstandings and tense feelings, the only way to make the situation work and have the living conditions remain palatable for everyone is to face the fact this this isn't easy, and work together as a group to find a solution.

TOUGH TIMES ON THE STREET/TRAVEL PATTERNS

On the streets or while traveling on mass transit, you may encounter someone who is visibly angry with no context relating back to you. They might be spewing negative or violent language into the air, or might even take a half-step in your direction to add emphasis to their diatribe. Of course they need help, and probably counseling. Many passersby will automatically drop their heads, practicing social avoidance and totally plugging out from someone exhibiting this kind of problem. But if someone in your general area is angry and acting unbalanced, is that what you really want to do? Lose sight and facing with them?

You should always keep your facing in these situations, even if just by turning your hips in their direction as you continue forward. Maybe you'll display a smile, have a kind word for them, or say nothing at all. But going into a temporary shell, acting as if this person is not there, both puts you at a tactical disadvantage and tends to further dehumanize them.

Ever been pickpocketed? Have someone reach into your back pocket, backpack, gym bag, or handbag to steal your wallet, money, or cell phone? It happens a lot on crowded streets. The culprit may have even been working with someone else who was there to distract you, perhaps by *accidentally* bumping into you and taking you off balance for a moment so you couldn't feel the theft.

Experts will tell you that you should carry your wallet and other valuables in your front pocket or a bag hanging down in front of you instead of on your shoulder or back. Imagine a pickpocket trying to steal from your front pocket while you have perfect facing. On the surface, it seems incredibly unlikely.

In airports, both Transportation Security Administration (TSA) and Homeland Security Investigations (HIS) officers use a type of facing when watching for individuals who may be involved in illicit activities such as smuggling. These experts at the art of observance take in someone's visage as a whole, watching to see if they're nervous, sweating, acting overly friendly, and speaking on their phones or texting at a time when others aren't. They're interpreting body language and looking for passengers with odd travel histories who stand out from the normal patterns.

NATURAL KUNG FU: GOING UP!

Learning Kung Fu has often been compared to climbing the face of a steep mountain. It can take great time, effort, and focus to get a substantial foothold on the art.

Kayla Greenberg, who played a myriad of different sports growing up, understands all about ascending to greater heights. By day, Kayla is a special education teacher. After school and during the summers, she's a climbing coach, teaching her clients how to scale rock walls, which can be as high as sixty feet.

Of course, Kayla had to face down her own obstacles in taking on such an assignment.

"My story is rather unique in the climbing world. I have a fear of heights," noted Kayla, who as a novice climber had a bad

Facing and Helping Hands

experience with the belayer (the person spotting her on a climb, holding the safety rope). "I went up the wall, the world suddenly got too small. I called to my belayer, 'Let me down! Let me down!' And instead, he kept on trying to push me to climb. I lost a lot of trust over that."

That's why Kayla is so well attuned to the personal apprehensions of new climbers.

"'It's way too tall. I could never climb to the top,' is what most of them tell me in the beginning," said Kayla. "I try to teach them to look at the bigger picture by breaking it down into smaller steps and setting goals. 'You're the climber. This is your wall. Your challenge. You don't need to get all the way up there today,' I tell them. Every climber is unique. And I want them to have an individualized climbing experience."

Kayla and one of her newest clients were both wonderfully impacted by such an individual experience on the wall.

"A young boy signed up for my class. Instantly, I could see that he had great movement and a natural technique on the rock, climbing right up to the top. So I praised him and told him to keep on climbing. The next session, he said, 'You gave me a compliment the other day, and said I was pretty good at climbing. I didn't know if you meant it or not. You see, I go to a special school. I have a learning disability. I've never been good at something before.'"

It was an emotional and intensely rewarding moment for Kayla.

"That really changed my perspective on what climbing and succeeding at something can bring to the lives of people," she recounted. "I feel really privileged to be a part of that."

Three cheers for Coach Kayla and all of her climbers!

[139]

Live Life Like a Kung Fu Master

PAUL'S PERSPECTIVE: THE SUBSTITUTE

During the years that I taught incarcerated teens on Rikers Island, occasionally one of my fellow educators would call in sick. That meant the NYC DOE would send a substitute teacher. There was a confirmed list of subs who had worked in the jail before, but every now and then a total newbie to the scene would be assigned. And if you think about the hard times you and your classmates gave to substitute teachers at your local high school, imagine that playing out behind bars, especially if the teacher has no experience in that system.

One day, a sub showed up late and was forced to walk into a classroom before any of the other teachers had a chance to prep him for what he might experience—how the teenage students, who were technically inmates, might try to maneuver him for gifts or favors. The rest of us worried that teacher wasn't schooled on either how to keep his *professional facing* relative to the students or what he might be *facing* as the teens sensed his newness.

Another teacher sat in the back of the room doing paperwork during that sub's first class, and gave us a thumbs-up that he seemed pretty sensible and able to take care of himself. That was important to the rest of the staff. Why? Well, we didn't want the students to ever get a taste of being in control because that would mostly leak over to our time with them, leaving us to quell any nonsense that had arisen and cutting into our teaching time.

Just before lunch, another teacher and I were chatting in the hallway, watching that sub work through a huge plastic window built into the side of each classroom's wall. That's when a student pointed at the watch the sub was wearing. We could basically read the student's lips. *Hey, that's a nice watch. Can I see it?* The sub foolishly took off his watch and handed it to the student. Like clockwork, there was a disturbance on the other side of the room, capturing the sub's attention, turning away from the

Facing and Helping Hands

student holding his watch. The watch was quickly handed off to a second student who buried it deep in his pocket.

The other teacher and I quickly entered the room and retrieved the watch for the sub. The students were banking on the idea that the sub would be too embarrassed to report that his watch had gone missing.

At lunch, several teachers gave that sub a quick lesson on how to maintain his facing in a jailhouse schoolroom. And as he headed over to his next classroom, I called out to him, "You know what? That really *is* a nice watch!"

LIFE APPLICATIONS

- Someone gives you a tip on a stock that they believe is about to rise in value. Instead of blindly investing your hard-earned money, you do your due diligence first, researching the company and watching market trends before you make a decision on whether or not to purchase the stock.
- You've been given the assignment of guarding the other team's best player one-on-one. So you focus on keeping your facing, shadowing your assigned player everywhere, cutting them off from getting into an effective position.
- Correctly budgeting your finances is something very important to you and your family. The early part of each month starts out with you and your partner keeping within the limits you both established. But upon reflection, you note that as each month passes, you get distracted by your kids' events, dinner invitations from friends, and other unexpected expenses. This month, however, you pledge not to lose sight of your budgetary goal.
- You're on a hiking trail for the first time. Though most of the trail is marked, some spots aren't. So you decide

to track your progress using an app on your phone that displays your position as you hike the trail.

I like a director who is very observant and is watching what I'm doing . . . but is giving me time to figure it out.
— Julia Stiles, actress

HONORED GUEST: SIFU JULIE ANN (CHELSEA/NEW YORK)

Sifu Julie Ann is a consummate New Yorker; she hasn't been hardened past the point of graciousness and civility by the city's streets. Rather, she's become acutely attuned to the often unpredictable surroundings, anchored by her confidence in herself, the people around her and, of course, her Kung Fu.

"I've been riding the subway since I was thirteen years old. I actually used to carry a large fork as a form of legal protection. I was scared a good part of my childhood. But as an adult and a trained martial artist, I no longer fear confrontation." A longtime practitioner of Eagle Claw Kung Fu (*Ying Jow Pai*), and part-owner of the Manhattan-based North Sky Kung Fu school, she continued, "Kung Fu helps you to avoid conflict in your daily life. It encourages you to always be in the present, and that provides you with an awareness. It's mind and body working together."

How can the art manifest itself in daily life?

"I think it provides me and a lot of practitioners with patience. Part of Kung Fu's translation is 'hard work and time.' So patience is something that martial artists develop and understand. Patience can teach you to observe a difficult situation and not overreact. That's something you learn in both training and fighting."

(continued next page)

Facing and Helping Hands

A graduate of New York's High School of Music & Art (now LaGuardia High School of Music & Art), where she excelled in both disciplines, Sifu Julie Ann eventually found Kung Fu, studying under famed Grandmaster Shum Leung, who shared a close friendship with Moy Yat.

"The mastery of the techniques in Eagle Claw Kung Fu—that's a treasure. There are so many riches to be gained from the system. But it can take massive time and effort to truly attain them. Students who are artists or possess a high-level of skill at something in their lives are often drawn to this system. They understand commitment. Many of my students are artists, musicians, and chess players."

Weapons training is also an integral part of Eagle Claw Kung Fu. Though no teacher expects their students to get into a street conflict with a traditional weapon such as a staff or a pole, the skills learned through such training can provide great benefits.

"Every weapon develops a skill in a practitioner that they can transfer into their life. There's eye-hand coordination and turning (with longer weapons), which can provide a three hundred and sixty-degree awareness of what's around you," said Sifu Julie Ann, who has personally developed an expertise in wielding a hand fan as a means of self-defense. "In real-life situations, an umbrella or cane can take the place of smaller weapons, providing a type of training that can really improve your footwork."

Why does Sifu Julie Ann believe that Kung Fu is so practical for our modern times?

"Yes, it teaches you to improve your confrontational abilities. But it also teaches you how to avoid confrontation, and that there's no shame in walking—or even running—away from a potential fight," she said. "Kung Fu is a journey that never ends."

[143]

CHAPTER THIRTEEN

BODY UNITY (*CHUM KIU*)

When spiders unite, they can tie down a lion.
—Ethiopian proverb

WHEN WE ARE UNIFIED in our thoughts and actions, we tend to be more confident in our ultimate direction. When our hearts and minds are in sync, even great labors don't deter us from our goals. That's the same type of cohesive momentum that can enable our bodies to perform at a level far beyond what we had initially envisioned for ourselves.

PHYSICAL ATTRIBUTES

The second of Wing Chun's open-handed forms, *Chum Kiu*, puts many of the foundational techniques of *Siu Nim Tao* into motion, with an emphasis on hand and body unity, footwork, and achieving dynamic balance. *Chum Kiu* translates as *seeking the bridge or sinking the bridge*. The "bridge" is the path to a contact point with the opponent, normally an arm or forearm, from which the Kung

Fu practitioner can feel the movements, or impending movements, of the opponent and either apply the proper technique or assume a superior position.

Chum Kiu teaches the practitioner to develop significant power through forward momentum, turning momentum, and pulling momentum. It stresses a connectivity to the ground and unison of movement between the hands and the body as potential power sources. The form puts both hands into play by combining techniques such as a *bong sau, wu sau* (creating one of several different two-handed techniques called *kwan sau*), and two simultaneous downward *bong saus* called *di bong sau*. Through the techniques presented in *Chum Kiu*, coupled with movement, the practitioner can seek a bridge to the opponent where one has yet to be established.

The *lan sau* or bar arm debuts in Chum Kiu through its ability to create a bridge. It is a jamming technique that evolves from a *bong sau* position. However, in the *lan sau*, the forearm is level with the shoulder and parallel to the body with an upward rotation. The technique can be used to create space or deliver a strike.

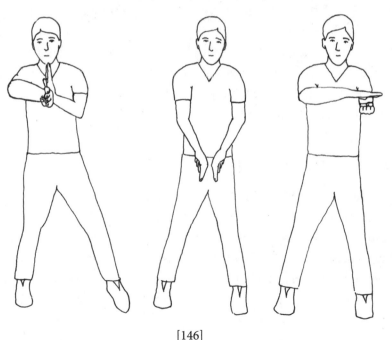

Body Unity (Chum Kiu)

The form further introduces the practitioner to a pair of kicks: the front kick (*dim gerk*) and the side kick (*wang gerk*). The multipurpose front kick can be used as a powerful offensive weapon or to block incoming kicks, often contacting the opponent's vulnerable shin. Both kicks are designed to be delivered to targets below the waist. And like Wing Chun's punches, the system's kicks do not compromise the practitioner's balance if the target is missed.

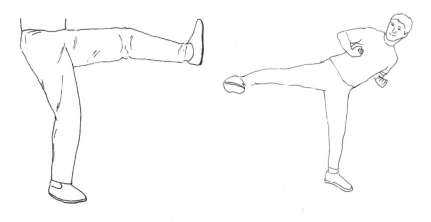

For a visual demonstration, go to YouTube and search: "Live Life Like a Kung Fu Master William Moy, Demonstrating Chum Kiu Form."

FROM MY LIFE: PRYING OPEN THE OYSTER

In 1953, my father was fifteen years old. He had just moved from Canton, China, to Hong Kong. His was a story similar to that of many other immigrants leaving mainland China, which was under the communist rule of leader Mao Zedong, all with hope of more freedom and a chance at greater economic prosperity in Hong Kong (which, at the time, was under British rule).

Live Life Like a Kung Fu Master

The surrounding world was in a state of flux. General Dwight D. Eisenhower had been sworn in as the US's thirty-fourth president (there were only forty-eight US states at the time). Elizabeth II had just ascended to the throne in Great Britain, Nikita Khrushchev was coming into power in the Soviet Union, and Fidel Castro was gaining control of Cuba.

It was only eight years after the end of World War II, and much of Asia was reeling economically, with vast numbers of unemployed citizenry.

Immediately upon his arrival in Hong Kong, my father began searching for a job to help his family. But being young and inexperienced, work was not so easy to find.

Aside from the daily act of going from shop to shop looking for owners who needed help, employment agencies were places that my father frequented in his search. He began to arrive at these hiring halls early in the morning, before they officially opened, in order to secure a place in line. My father would wait outside with hundreds of other people, trying to get an edge on the competition.

When the doors of the agency would open, everyone would rush into a big hall, waiting for the first clerk to appear with a job slip to announce an opening. My father had witnessed this for several days—the few who succeeded and the many who failed to walk away with something.

But on this particular morning, my father decided that he needed to be more self-promoting.

As the clerk emerged from the office, even before he began to read the job description from the slip, my father's arm shot up, screaming, "I'll take it! I'll take it!" Leaping to his feet, my father snatched the slip from the clerk's hand and was on his way to his first job in a new land. It didn't matter that he didn't know what or where it was. He was creating his own momentum toward success.

[148]

Chum Kiu means *seeking the bridge*. It entails actively looking for something, a connection to the opponent in terms of fighting. But this concept will serve you well in many other aspects of life.

Your actions will need to be direct and clear, just as those of my father were in that employment agency. The type of job being offered was irrelevant to him. As a young man with still a lot to learn, he was hungry to acquire new skills to achieve a better life. If others wouldn't train him, then he would train himself. Studying and reading were among his personal pursuits. For my father, dashing to that slip of paper first was the bridge to the other side.

> *What is great in man is that he is a bridge and not a goal.*
> —Friedrich Nietzsche, German philosopher

UNIFIED MOTION IN SOCIETY/SPORTS

The dynamic lessons of *Chum Kiu*'s ability to connect with others and generate power from a unified, rhythmic body in motion fully has its parallels in the world around us.

Consider the protest movements for women's rights, civil rights, and various other causes stretching back from the mid-nineteenth century to today. Bring a body of people together in support of the same beliefs and their unification will make them stronger as a whole than any individual voice. Put them in motion, perhaps on a protest march or an economic boycott, and their actions will most likely create a bridge to others of similar or dissimilar minds, creating connections, dialogue, and debate.

Workers on a picket line striking for better pay and conditions find greater strength through coordinated activities. Just consider the meaning of the word *union*. It is defined as "the act of being joined, or an association of those with common interests."

Live Life Like a Kung Fu Master

In an election, multiple candidates and their supporting bodies are in motion to wage a campaign. Their goal is to connect to others, creating a bridge of support that can carry them to victory at the polls.

Consider all the moving parts of a high school or college marching band, whether during halftime of a football game or as part of a parade down Main Street. From the drum majors to the woodwind, brass, and percussion members, their performance—both physically and rhythmically—forges a connection to the audience.

The dynamic stance of a skier going down a slope constantly changes to adapt to a myriad of forces, including the terrain and their desired speed. Balance is key, and the skier's back—like that of a Kung Fu practitioner—is almost always neutral. As in Wing Chun, skiers form a triangle with the lower half of their bodies, using the ankles, knees, and hips to supply structural integrity, power, and control.

Now watch a weightlifter perform a clean and press as they do in the Olympics. At the instant the weight is brought to the "clean" position upon their chests, there's a unified outward rotating of the shoulders and hips. The feet, as in Kung Fu, are gripping the floor as a source of power, with the balance point being the middle of the sole. It takes a body in spectacular concert to achieve the weighty task of the "clean," and that's even before the motion of the "press" occurs. Naturally, strength without polished technique falters in this arena.

NATURAL KUNG FU: DANCING AND BODY UNITY

In many ways, *Chum Kiu* resembles a well-choreographed dance, with the practitioner moving across the ground, galvanizing upper and lower body movements in rhythm to one another. Interestingly, Bruce Lee competed in and won cha-cha

Body Unity (Chum Kiu)

tournaments, while Moy Yat was an accomplished ballroom dancer.

Susan McGreevy-Nichols is the executive director of the National Dance Education Organization, which promotes dance in all forms to students nationwide. For nearly four decades, Susan, a natural choreographer who sees the movements in her mind before they're a reality on the floor, has been inspiring students to make dance part of their lives.

"It's both a physical exercise and an art form," said McGreevy-Nichols. "It takes lots of cognitive processes to create and then learn a choreographed dance piece."

Dancing and martial arts have long gone hand in hand, with many ballet dancers, both male and female, engaging in martial arts training.

"I had a student who was a boxer begin to study dance. He was trying out for the Junior Olympic Team, and believed that his time in dance helped his footwork as a boxer a great deal," recalled McGreevy-Nichols.

Is there a connection between prearranged dance steps and learning a martial arts form?

"Absolutely. To become a better performer, first you have to learn the piece and make it a part of yourself through muscle memory," said McGreevy-Nichols. "Only then can you work on all of the little details, and get feedback from someone such as a teacher. The art of dance promotes body unity. It creates it through the act of choreography, which in reality is a form of problem solving, getting the body to move in unison, resulting in efficiency, and clarity of expression."

LIFE APPLICATIONS

- The walking path in the local park gets flooded after a heavy rainstorm. In response, someone has taken a pair

of wooden planks and stretched them across the area that normally floods to serve as a makeshift bridge.
- You attend a friend's party at which most of the guests are strangers to you. Taking it upon yourself to make connections, you introduce yourself to various people there, asking about their lives and telling them about your own.
- You've developed a wicked slice at ping pong by timing the rotation of your shoulder and wrist with the instant you make contact with the ball.
- As your child turns the page of a pop-up book, the mechanisms that control the different features—stage set, v-fold, box and cylinder, and floating layers—work in unison to create a captivating motion-filled multi-image.

Unity is vision; it must have been part of the process of learning to see.

—Henry Adams

HAMMERIN' HANK
When Henry "Hank" Aaron retired from baseball in 1976, he was the all-time home run king, having hit 755 homers during his illustrious twenty-three-year career. It didn't matter that the right-handed hitting native of Mobile, Alabama, stood six feet tall and weighed just 180 pounds. Yes, there were bigger and stronger players than Aaron. But that didn't matter. Aaron's technique at the plate was spectacular. And though he wasn't a practicing martial artist, Aaron was a model of Kung Fu consistency, melding multiple power sources in immaculate rhythm to send baseballs flying beyond the fences.

How did Hank Aaron do it?

(continued next page)

Body Unity (Chum Kiu)

An instant before starting his swing, Aaron dipped the barrel of the bat toward home plate. It was a trigger mechanism to get his timing and structure perfectly aligned. Aaron was known for his huge and powerful wrists. Upon contacting his bat with the baseball, Aaron turned his top wrist over, creating immense torque. This also enabled him to create a flat bat path in which he was able to hit fastballs at the top of the strike zone. His hitting structure produced more line drives without purposely trying to undercut a pitch, adding loft. The result was like hitting the baseball on the button with a hammer instead of a bat, all due to Aaron's ability to synchronize his entire body into one seemingly complete motion.

CHAPTER FOURTEEN

Creating Leverage for Ourselves

The most common way people give up their power is by thinking they don't have any.

—Alice Walker, author

LEVERAGE ISN'T SOMETHING WE should wield over others to feed our egos. It's a mechanical concept that often plays out professionally, socially, and societally. In all of its forms, leverage is there to enhance our lives and be a stepping stone to a more productive life.

PHYSICAL ATTRIBUTES

Kung Fu, and Wing Chun in particular as a system devised by a woman, focuses on using leverage over brute strength, enabling someone smaller and weaker to dispatch a larger opponent. Its implementation is a study in Physics 101. Kung Fu derives much of its power source from using the mechanical advantage of turning the human body into multiple levers. That concepts further amplified through the correct positioning and alignment of its foundational techniques and applied angles. Elbows, wrists, hips, and knees are essential allies in creating leverage, as well as being firmly rooted to the ground so the practitioner can dissipate an incoming force.

Here's an example of using leverage in the system: Make a *bong sau* using your right arm, then have someone play a mock opponent (facing you), putting their extended left arm on top of your fully formed technique, with their fist reaching just an inch or two beyond the center of your *bong sau* (normally, your left hand would be in a *wu sau* as a backup behind your *bong sau*, because we always want to keep two hands active and alive). Now drop your right elbow downward, using it as a fulcrum point to turn your *bong sau* into a *tan sau*. That simple movement will swing the opposing punch off the center and open a clear path for you to use your elbow as a lever to deliver a punch or palm strike to the target area.

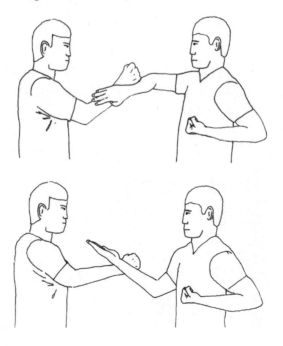

On a front kick (*dim gerk*), the knee is lifted until it is parallel with the hip, making your thigh a virtual tabletop, extending from your hip to the elevated knee. As the kick thrusts forward with the heel as a striking point on the center line, you are creating leverage with a trio of joints—hip, knee, and ankle—adding to the front kick's essential power.

For a visual demonstration, go to YouTube and search: "Live Life Like a Kung Fu Master—William Moy, Demonstrating Leverage."

FROM MY LIFE: ARTISTIC LEVERAGE

One of the ways to create leverage is be armed with all the information available. To this purpose, the Wing Chun system has a technique called *mon sau* or *asking hands*. It's accomplished by extending your arms to the farthest reach possible, in a sweeping, upward motion. It's not meant as an attack, but rather more of a probe to receive and interpret information.

I've used the concept of *mon sau* many times in my life without ever physically lifting my arms. My goal was generally to feel out an unfolding situation with my words, facial expression, or other nonthreatening physical actions, in the hopes of placing myself in the best position possible.

Live Life Like a Kung Fu Master

Once, as a skinny teen, when I was convinced two guys on a New York City subway had intentions of robbing me, I actually turned my jacket pockets inside out and announced, "Look, I have no money." That gave them the information they needed, and the situation abated.

During the seventh grade, I became focused on being accepted into the specialized High School of Art and Design in Manhattan, which boasts a long list of prominent artists from many fields as alumni. The school is renowned for its top-notch art classes, something that had my complete interest. I had a best friend whose older brother had graduated from the school. My friend and I, another budding artist, would marvel at his brother's pencil drawings, and hoped to study in the same program.

Admission to the school wasn't easy. There was a citywide test you needed to pass, which offered limited seats to its many applicants. Beginning almost two years prior to that test, I began to gather the experience necessary to prove myself. I rigorously explored many genres of drawing and painting, including charcoal, oil paints, and watercolors. I would volunteer for everything around my junior high that needed some kind of art work. Whether it was painting murals on the school walls, creating scenery for the school play, or designing posters for a variety of causes and events, the teachers—and especially my art teacher—knew that they could count on me to produce something worthy.

Finally, the day arrived to take the test. I walked through the impressive doors of that famed high school dreaming of everything I could accomplish there. I was a little nervous and, in my memory, the whole process of being interviewed and taking the test seemed like a blur.

I was notified by mail a week later. The next day at school, upon hearing that the results had been released, my art teacher congratulated me on getting in. I sadly had to explain that I

Creating Leverage for Ourselves

wasn't chosen. My art teacher, rather annoyed with the news, said to me, "I'm going to have to make a call."

I didn't really know what that meant at the time but, several days later, I was accepted to Art and Design. It seems that the selection committee always holds several additional seats open for talented students that they've either missed or possibly misjudged.

"This isn't special treatment. It had nothing to do with me. You honestly deserve this opportunity. I just helped to open their eyes about who you are and what you've accomplished," said my art teacher, as we both celebrated my acceptance.

Looking back on it now, I see that through my hard work and dedication to art and the school, I had created my own form of leverage. And that leverage inspired a teacher to put their reputation on the line for me. My art teacher had all of the information on me as an artist, gleaned over the previous two years, and simply made sure the depth of that information became available to the selection committee, too.

Knowledge is love and light and vision.

—Helen Keller

IN OUR LIVES

We often create leverage for ourselves at our jobs. Perhaps we're the only ones who can perform a certain task. The only employee who can speak several languages. The lone salesperson who has a good relationship with a major client. Or even the only one who can fix the copy machine to avoid another service call by the manufacturer (simply hit it with your hip three degrees before dead center). And we're all familiar with the running joke that the IT department seemingly runs many Fortune 500 companies because the other employees, supervisors, and executives, as a

Live Life Like a Kung Fu Master

whole, are not as tech savvy. When the system goes down and nothing can get done, who are you going to call? I-T!

The best way to create leverage is to have knowledge of a situation. The more knowledge that you possess, the more you can separate yourself from the pack and stand out. Of course, you may also choose to share your knowledge with others, becoming a pivot point or fulcrum for them to exert leverage. That makes you ultra valuable to the team. In fact, it's a quality in which many of the world's most recognized business executives, military leaders, government employees, coaches, and teachers pride themselves on.

Banks have the financial leverage of having cash on hand when they either give you a loan or a mortgage, charging you interest. Businesses have something called operating leverage, when their profits go up but their costs remain the same.

We're all interested in leveraging our time, undoubtedly our most precious resource. We make schedules for ourselves and determine which activities are the most vital to our success or well-being. Study. Exercise. Social engagements. Family activities. What will be your motivations to decide how much time to allot for each?

Consider a football coach whose team is already ahead on the scoreboard by sixteen points with just a few minutes remaining on the game clock. In calling the offensive plays from the sideline that coach simply wants to keep the clock moving. Scoring more points is currently lower on the list of priorities. That team would rather leverage time by trying to run out the clock. Meanwhile, on the other sideline, the opposing coach is using the remaining time outs in order to leverage their ability to preserve time.

We also use leverage in our relationships. Whom do we want around us? Will those individuals or groups help us to grow and bring positivity into our lives? And are there other people in our lives from whom we need to distance ourselves? Having all of the information will help you to decide.

Creating Leverage for Ourselves

NATURAL KUNG FU: A PITCHING PIONEER

During her career as a professional baseball player, Ila Borders, who broke the barrier as the first female pitcher to start and win a men's professional game, displayed an abundance of natural Kung Fu. She accomplished the feat in 1998 while pitching in the minor leagues for the Duluth-Superior Dukes. Standing 5-foot-9 and weighing 150 pounds, Ila, competing against much bigger and stronger men, used leverage and positioning (pitch placement) to overcome the physical disadvantage.

"I'd break down my movements. I really had to be in tune with my body to get every inch of power out of this five-nine frame. I'd even make sure to push off the mound using my big toe to produce more power. My fastball topped out at about 83 or 84 miles per hour, but I'd position it correctly at the right time, either on the outside corner of home plate or up and in to the batter. Some pitchers throw at 90 miles per hour. Only if it's over the middle of the plate, they're going to get hit anyway," said the left-handed throwing Borders, who pitched in Little League, high school, and college, receiving a full athletic scholarship to Southern California College (now Vanguard University of Southern California).

Throughout her playing career, Borders faced plenty of outside pressures, which needed to be redirected elsewhere if she was going to succeed. "I talk about developing sustained discipline, eliminating distractions, and knowing what distracts you. Instead of allowing those things to cause fear and hurt my performance, I turned them into fuel to give me strength. People have yelled at me, cursed at me, been hostile in numerous ways, and even thrown beer at me in minor league ballparks," recalled Borders. "I didn't allow it to deter me because I had a strong purpose in my life. I was meant to do something—to become the first woman to pitch in men's professional baseball and be the best at it."

Besides passionately chasing her own dream, Borders was building bridges through her baseball career. "Maybe I didn't

[161]

realize it back then, but I realize it now. That's the part that I feel really good about, building those bridges and being able to connect with people. I wouldn't go home after a game until I signed every ball for every kid. That was a responsibility to me," said Borders, who believes she has inspired many young girls, as well as boys, to chase their dreams.

When her playing career was over, Ila built societal bridges in another way, by coming out as gay. "Coming out and telling people my story was extremely scary for me. I thought I'd lose my friends and family. But it's also building bridges because other people will say, 'Ila has done it, I can do it, too.' Hopefully, if I can get one person to have more courage in themselves, then that's a win for everyone."

Today, Ila is a full-time firefighter/paramedic in Oregon, holding the rank of captain. "I get to help people, sometimes on the worst day of their lives. For me, it's the best job in the world—along with baseball."

LIFE APPLICATIONS

- Every morning you ask both Siri and Google about the weather outside. The information is helpful, but you never decide if you'll take a jacket with you on your commute to work until after you've walked the dog and experienced what's going on for yourself.
- You use a wheelbarrow to move fifty pounds of dirt from your backyard to your front yard by creating upward leverage on the wheelbarrow's handles, with the single wheel acting as a fulcrum.
- You ask for a raise in pay, pushing the fact that last month you landed a major account for your firm that now comprises almost 20 percent of the total business revenue.

- The same way you use a screwdriver to turn a screw, you use your Kung Fu to lessen life's heavier loads.

Creativity is the power to connect the seemingly unconnected.
—William Plomer, South African/British novelist and poet

ONE BODY, ONE INCH

Jessica Rose, a current Professor of Orthopedic Surgery at Stanford University, conducted a 2014 study (when she was a biomechanical researcher at that same institution) on Wing Chun Kung Fu's legendary one-inch punch. She chose the most famous example of the shockingly power-packed blow, performed by Bruce Lee at a Long Beach, California, martial arts event in 1964.

But how could the power to knock an opponent back several yards be generated in the space of just one inch? According to Rose's findings, after examining the grainy black and white film of the blow in question, it's all about coordination and timing combined with the power of leverage.

It starts with the ground and ankles, right before the extension of Lee's knees, as he stands in one spot with his arm almost fully extended. In nearly the same motion, his hips twist and shoulder thrusts. Then the elbow, amplifying that leverage, surges forward. Finally, there's a flick of the wrist. By leveraging the coordinated force of nearly the entire body into a tiny area, and then pulling back almost immediately upon impact, thereby compressing the applied force even further, the one-inch punch finds its incredible power . . . and appropriately so for a close-range fighting system such as Wing Chun.

You may familiar with a scene from the film *Kill Bill: Volume 2*, in which the character (The Bride) being

(continued next page)

Live Life Like a Kung Fu Master

played by actress Uma Thurman uses a one inch to escape a buried coffin. It's interesting to note that little of Professor Rose's findings are applicable here to support such power in a punch because the dynamics and positioning (being horizontal) are so different. Well, it *is* the movies.

CHAPTER FIFTEEN

A MODEL OF EFFICIENCY

Time stays long enough for anyone who will use it.
—Leonardo de Vinci, Italian polymath

BEING EFFICIENT IN BOTH our personal and professional lives is a quality in which we can all strive to master. That's because the reward can be something incredibly valuable and meaningful to everyone: time not wasted.

PHYSICAL ATTRIBUTES

Kung Fu, and in particular Wing Chun, is a model of martial arts efficiency. Because Wing Chun is a short-range fighting system of strikes, kicks, and techniques to unbalance your opponent, it is designed for the practitioner to first arrive at the target area, which is on your center line. The optimal way to do that is to be straight and direct, without detours or bends. Wing Chun chain punches (*yat jechung choi*) embody this principle, churning like the pistons in a finely turned engine, turning one over top the other with neither the right nor left hand/fist ever leaving the

[165]

center line. This will give the practitioner a concerted edge over an opponent whose strikes either travel a great distance or need to be pulled back to gather sufficient momentum. In fact, the chain punches are so efficient that they are always ready to move forward from their current position without ever traveling away from the target (rearing back).

We also never defend outside of the boundary line of our body. For example, the *pak* or block in *Siu Nim Tao* extends to the length of our right and left shoulder blade (making the block with the opposite hand) and no more. This type of efficiency is further displayed by the Wing Chun system being designed to never chase the opponent's hand. Rather, we remain focused on chasing their center. If an opponent's strike is on the center, we might meet it there—either by blocking and returning pressure with a *pak da*. We can also strike through it by locking it down with the bottom of our extended forearm and turning our single straight punch into an ultraefficient combined block/strike, getting two results in one movement.

A Model of Efficiency

FROM MY LIFE: AN UNFADING SNAPSHOT

As I step back and look at my life, I see so much of my father's influence upon it, as well as the impact of the Kung Fu that he taught me. Efficiency, simplicity, straightforwardness, personal creativity, and being humble—those are among the cornerstones of the art, the kinds of qualities that can touch and guide your everyday existence.

Sometimes these qualities appear in the simple act of sitting down at a café, diner, or restaurant where the wait staff knows you by name. They seat you at your favorite table or booth whenever it's available. They automatically pour your coffee or tea because they already know how you like it served. And you can engage in personal conversations with them without needing to glance at their name tag.

My father was a master at being efficient. He made living a multifaceted life appear seamless, including maintaining a marvelous and loving relationship with my mother. Besides having a strong hand in raising me, he accomplished the same feat for my two sisters. But it didn't end there, as it often does with most other families. For my father had his extended Kung Fu family to consider daily. There were his martial arts brothers and sisters back in China, and most importantly, his sifu, Ip Man, who sadly passed away in 1972 at the age of seventy-nine. Then there were my father's students, the ones who lived in New York City and trained under his guidance several times per week. There were also the students who had moved on to different parts of the US and the world, but still turned to him for advice or in celebration of an achievement in their lives.

And yet with all of that, I can't remember a single, clear instance when my father seemed pressed for time or overwhelmed by life.

Adding to it all, my father remained a dedicated artist—painting and drawing up until his final days. He somehow lived a fast-paced life while taking up permanent residence in the slow lane. Instead of people reacting with a honk of their horn for him to speed up, the individuals with whom he came into contact for any length of time, especially his students, slowed themselves down to join him on his Kung Fu–fueled journey.

In my mind's eye, I can still see my father arriving at his favorite Chinatown restaurant for a Saturday afternoon lunch, usually after teaching a morning class. He would arrive with several of his students in tow, waiting to discuss the just-concluded lesson and the challenges of life they'd be facing in the upcoming week. A waiter would then show my father to his regular table before handing him his favorite newspaper. As my father begins to scan the headlines, he kept an open ear on the conversation of his students, breaking in to comment or provide an opinion only when necessary.

In many ways, it's a snapshot of Kung Fu Life that I'd be pleased to pass on to you.

> *Don't spend time beating on a wall, hoping to transform it into a door.*
>
> —Coco Chanel, businesswoman

PERSONAL EFFICIENCY

Perhaps you live life on a tight schedule. Your workweek is normally filled from top to bottom with commuting, meetings, clients, and other work-related duties. Your weekends also seem to be delineated by time slots such as chauffeuring the kids to their various activities, household repairs, grocery shopping, and doing laundry. No wonder you haven't the energy to separate each load of laundry by colors! But think about it. No one really *lives* on a schedule. It's just a guideline to keep us moving forward, a framework that conjures up the image of efficiency. But are you really efficient?

A Model of Efficiency

When you perform each activity, are you at your best? Are you completely focused? Is it possible that by doing fewer activities you could perform the ones you choose to do at a much higher level? I suppose it all depends on how you personally judge the notion of efficiency. If you've aligned your grocery shopping with dropping the kids off at their weekend activity, making one fewer car trip as a result, congratulations. That's a good bit of natural Kung Fu.

Lots of people, and the companies for which they're employed, discovered a new definition of efficiency during the COVID-19 pandemic. With more people working from home, and the time and energy saved via a lack of a commute, both employees and their employers got a glimpse of reevaluating the concept of efficiency. Which way did the pendulum swing? The University of Chicago researched the topic and concluded that non-commuting employees devoted approximately one-third of their saved commute time to their primary work assignments.

Kung Fu practitioners are recognized for keeping both hands alive, ready to produce a desired result at any moment with either appendage. They can also apply a three-pronged attack—using a two-handed technique as well as bringing a single leg into the mix, achieved through maintaining proper balance so that the remaining leg on the ground can adequately support the body. Can you achieve something like this in your family, social, or work-related life?

No one knows your life better than you. Instead of providing several abstract scenarios on how you can combine activities, in this chapter we'll leave the brainstorming in your capable hands. You were told early on in this text that Wing Chun was a self-correcting art and that, eventually, you would become your own sifu. Here's your opportunity to take an initial step in that direction.

Live Life Like a Kung Fu Master

NATURAL KUNG FU: STRIDING FORWARD

Oklahoma native Mark Elliston has been coaching track and field on the collegiate level for almost four decades. "Part of my job is to make the young men and women athletes whom I coach more efficient on the track. We each have a reserve of athletic talent and genetics with which we were born, and that's basically it. So becoming more efficient is one way to increase our performance," said Coach Elliston, who is the Director of Track and Field and Cross County at Elon University in North Carolina. "Becoming more efficient as a runner is a process. We look at things like body control, placement of the knee, the heel, running more upright, and, of course, being more relaxed."

Repetition and drills, often with weighted sleds and resistance bands, are used to create muscle memory for being in the correct position.

"There are biomechanical computer models that show the perfect stride for both sprinters and distance runners. We try to get our athletes as close as possible to that perfect model, whether we need to work on stride length, stride frequency or changing bad physical habits," said Elliston, who competed as a high jumper and decathlete in his time on the track.

Becoming too tense is something with which most of us can relate, especially during a big event. But running economically is incredibly difficult when athletes can't control their emotions.

"They'll grit their teeth and clench their fists, all in an attempt to run faster," observed Elliston. "They're just asking for fatigue to come on. I tell them, 'You're tensing muscles you don't even need to run.' What they really need is to trust more in the positions they've trained, and not have their brains override that."

In many ways, efficiency is discipline. When runners are faced with that challenging moment when they either take a step forward or regress, they're often near the point of physical and mental exhaustion.

"When their hearts are pounding and their lungs feel as if they're about to burst, that's when an athlete has to fight through it, to get to the other side of that challenging moment," said Elliston. "I have a definition for that kind of discipline: It's doing what you don't want to do, but has to be done."

Not every collegiate athlete is going to win an Olympic medal or turn pro, so the efficiency that coaches inspire in their performance is meant to win more than track meets. It's meant to help them in their future lives.

"I strongly encourage our athletes to take these tools into everyday life, especially on campus. To strive to be emotionally in control and to do well with their studies. As bad things happen, and life seems to be falling apart, they need to stay calm and take control of the things they can control," emphasized Coach Elliston, who possesses an extraordinary passion for positively affecting the lives of others.

PAUL'S PERSPECTIVE: THE PAGES OF TIME

This is my twenty-first book, and the third time I've had the pleasure of co-authoring a work with someone. Like most authors, being a professional writer wasn't my first job. I've pumped gas (back in the days when cars had gas caps and, occasionally, I'd forget to put one back on), loaded packages onto trucks at the depot for UPS during the Christmas rush (they wrote on my chart that I was unmotivated, and were probably correct), received a pair of aircraft mechanic licenses from the FAA (though I never did that as a job), taught English for the New York City Department of Education for sixteen years, and have been a credentialed reporter in the sport of thoroughbred racing since 1996.

That means I started writing books and acting as a professional writer before a major publisher was willing to pay me to do so. I wrote at night, sometimes most of the night, after working

Live Life Like a Kung Fu Master

my day job. To complicate matters, I had a wonderful loving family comprised of my wife April, daughter Sabrina, my parents, a pair of dogs, and a menagerie of smaller animals—all of whom needed and deserved my attention.

That's the juggle. How to realistically ration your time and best energies?

Of course, it doesn't need to be writing that has captured your attention. It could be music, drawing, painting, sculpture, dance, acting, starting a business—almost any passionate pursuit. You get serious about something and commit to it before there is ever any real recognition, just the satisfaction of doing what makes you feel more complete. And this kind of life-juggle demands that you become extremely efficient at budgeting your time and energy.

Almost all of the writers whom I've met over the past two decades share a single common denominator, as if it were part of their collective DNA. They are wholly efficient when it comes to carving out time to ply their craft, no matter what's going on in their lives.

I was already a professional writer when I became serious about studying Kung Fu. My wife had her doubts that I could juggle an additional pursuit, especially since I was playing basketball two nights a week as well. But though the art took up some valuable space in my already crowded schedule, I began to discover that Kung Fu provided me a good bit more in return.

The art improved my patience. It began to give me an overall better balance in life, helping me to feel and interpret more of what was going on around me. And though efficiency was absolutely among my strong points at the start of my Kung Fu journey, I feel as though the art refined that quality in me, providing a better perspective on how to judge meaningful time and distance.

I don't know how many more books will become a part of my writing career but, in sitting down with Sifu William for my

[172]

A Model of Efficiency

part in penning this one, it has reinforced in me why I believe possessing even a moderate amount of Kung Fu can be a valuable tool for anyone.

LIFE APPLICATIONS

- It's a beautiful fall day with the foliage along the side of the highway turning incredible shades of red and yellow. So you get out of the fast lane for a while to take in the view, confident that you will arrive at your destination in a better frame of mind, instead of fifteen minutes earlier.
- This weekend's weather forecast of possible showers has you slightly unnerved. That's because of the big backyard party you've scheduled, inviting a couple dozen family members, friends, and work colleagues. So you decide to focus on what you can control, and you make contingency plans to hold the event inside your home.
- The duplication of efforts in your workplace has always bothered you. Two people basically collect the same information from clients without any increase in productivity. So you devise a workable plan to free up the second employee to do other needed tasks.
- You create a new weekend schedule for yourself. It's one not ruled by the clock, but by the resulting quality of each endeavor you undertake.

I knew I could control one thing, and that is my time and my hours and my effort and my efficiency.
—Ryan Seacrest, media personality

Interestingly, the term "martial arts" doesn't find its roots in Asian culture. Rather, it gets its name from Mars, the Roman god of war, whose providence was also valued in securing peace through strength. It was common practice for Roman soldiers heading into battle to pray to Mars for victory. But, ultimately, the Romans believed it was Mars, emblematically represented by a sword and shield, who decided which side would triumph, not the skill of the soldiers or their earthly commanders. As Roman influence spread across Europe during the fifteenth century, Romans, in an attempt to describe their gladiatorial combat sports, both armed and unarmed, to other civilizations, initiated "martial arts" into the wider lexicon.

Among the brightest objects in our night sky, the fourth planet from our sun was named Mars by the Romans, in honor of their god. In ancient Asian cultures, the luminous planet was referred to as the "fire star."

HONORED GUEST: COACH GREG ARDON (BROOKLYN/EL SALVADOR)

Adolescents often need to convince their parents to allow them to study martial arts. But that wasn't the case for champion martial artist Greg Ardon, founder and head coach of Ardon Sweet Science Gym in Brooklyn, New York. Greg's beloved mother, Esther Ardon, whom he sadly lost in 2023, was a dedicated fan of martial arts films and encouraged her son to begin his study.

"She was a huge fan of Kung Fu movies. Bruce Lee was her favorite, her absolute screen hero. She

(continued next page)

A Model of Efficiency

thought that one day, especially because we were relatively the same size and weight, I could be like him," said Coach Ardon, whose family immigrated to the US from El Salvador, and who, by the age of nineteen, had already won the Four Star Full-Contact Kung Fu world championship in San Francisco, California. "When I was younger, she would come to watch me play soccer. Sometimes there would be an *accidental* kick on a player instead of the ball, usually on me, and a fight would break out. It happened enough that she enrolled me in Kung Fu class."

Ardon began his martial arts journey by studying Fu Jow Pai Kung Fu under the tutelage of Grandmaster Wai Hong. Later on, Ardon studied boxing and Muay Thai kickboxing, eventually winning the New York State and National Full-Contact Championships.

Greg's grandfather, Moises Ardon, always encouraged him to share his martial knowledge with others. And he was a driving force in getting his grandson to open his own business, with Ardon Sweet Science Gym becoming a reality at the start of 2005. Since that time, Ardon has gotten many young Brooklynites away from the negative influences of the street and into boxing and other forms of self-defense. He also assisted in the training of Oscar-winning actress Hilary Swank, preparing her to box for the film *Million Dollar Baby* (2004).

As the gym's head coach, Ardon not only brings his own competitive experience to his trainees, but he also has a degree in sports psychology from the City College of New York. "My background and education helps me to better understand the athletes whom I train—their overall mentality, why they've come to train, their anxieties, and how I can view and reach each of them as an individual," said Ardon.

Now in his fifties, Ardon has taken a keen interest in Wing Chun over the last several years, studying with

(continued next page)

Live Life Like a Kung Fu Master

Sifu William "I like William's approach. He's very laid back and relaxed, always explaining the philosophy and mechanics behind each technique," said Ardon. "I think Wing Chun is a good complement to my other martial skills. Together, they're very harmonious. This style of Kung Fu has a calm nature about it. I like to incorporate the Yin and Yang philosophy or 'soft and hard' into everything I do. If there's a fight coming your way, try to talk your way out of it first. It's about having control of your emotions. Both Wing Chun and working with William have strongly influenced me in that way."

CHAPTER SIXTEEN

EGO IS THE ENEMY

The ego is not master in its own house.
—Dr. Sigmund Freud

WHAT IS EGO? EGO is defined as a person's sense of self-esteem or self-importance. That's an interesting combination, and a fine line for someone to walk. Most of us have experienced, either in ourselves or others, when one's sense of self-importance overrides the value of a positive sense of self-esteem—and the results can usually be quite a turnoff.

PHYSICAL ATTRIBUTES

Possessing an ego is exceedingly normal. As internal motivation, it can be partly responsible for our success in achieving many of the goals we set for ourselves. It pushes us to strive to be the best at something. And it could be one of the driving forces that helps to pick us up off the ground and move forward after a perceived failure. The ego provides a sense of personal identity, helping us

Live Life Like a Kung Fu Master

navigate society as we waver between our innate desires and what our conscience tells us is socially acceptable behavior.

But it doesn't really require reading several volumes of Dr. Sigmund Freud, whose meticulous research on the human personality in the 1920s explained the complexities of the id, ego, and superego, for us to realize that when someone puts their inflated ego ahead of everything else, the end result is usually less than satisfying for the rest of us.

In a Kung Fu class, this type of ego-driven student might put others in danger by being overly aggressive during training exercises or be discouraging to classmates by downgrading their abilities, via verbal or physical cues. Since students normally learn from one another through a conduit that flows directly from the sifu, it's easy for that delicate balance to be disturbed. Inflated egotism is the type of behavior that needs to be addressed immediately by both the senior students and the sifu whenever it appears. Should it go on for too long, the younger students—or *si dai* of that individual—may perceive that this is acceptable behavior, in turn treating their own *si dai* in such a manner.

And what happens when a younger student acquires an amount of Kung Fu that surpasses their older brother or sister? Will ego creep in from either party and ruin the relationship?

One of the Wing Chun maxims states: Be humble to request your teacher for guidance.

And after your teacher demonstrates an exercise, a technique, or imparts some wisdom about the art of Kung Fu, the respectful and humble response on the part of the student or entire class is *Doje sifu gau do*, which translates as *Thank you teacher for the guidance*.

FROM MY LIFE: THE REUNIONS

I once overheard a Kung Fu brother of mine remark to someone, "It's interesting how William calls his father 'sifu' during

[178]

Ego is the Enemy

class." This brother actually lived in our home for a time, so he had heard me use the title "father" under different circumstances. Whenever I was in class, though, I remained extremely aware of wanting to be judged on my merits as a practitioner of the art and not as the sifu's son.

It would have been relative-ly (excuse the pun) easy, especially as a youngster searching for an identity, to use my father's position to bolster my sense of self-worth, at least in my own mind. Not that my father would have allowed it by any means.

There was a mantra among the students at the school: Leave your ego at the door. And I tried to follow it to the letter, so much so that I probably deferred to others on various occasions when I could have pursued my own preferences. Those were observations that served me well as a teen. But they served me even better when I became a sifu, with my own sons, Nicholas and Marcus, attending my class.

My Kung Fu brother, who seemed to be keeping track of how I addressed my father in different circumstances back then, struggled a bit with keeping his ego in check. Maybe that's why he was so concerned with my language, judging it against what he would have done.

I remember when he returned to class after an extremely long absence, one in which he was able to continue his martial studies in Hong Kong. Upon our reunion, he invited me to *chi sau* with him. I took it as a friendly gesture, one to celebrate our training together again.

Not long into that *chi sau* session, however, he attempted to strike me with an unorthodox technique, an elbow strike (*gwai jaang*) launched with full speed and force. It was something that a practitioner from our school would have never attempted without prior consent from their training partner, as well as testing it at a lower-intensity first.

I felt the tenseness of that strike building in his body through my contact reflexes. By the time he released that energy, I was a

Live Life Like a Kung Fu Master

half-step ahead of him, halting the progress of his elbow with a block and spinning him away from my center, while he remained on mine.

With his ego bruised beyond repair in that moment, he demanded to know how I anticipated his technique. I didn't need to fly sixteen hours abroad to learn how to defend that move.

"That's the type of Kung Fu that has always been here," I said, in a low-key tone. "You just never realized it."

I didn't see him for a while after that exchange. But, eventually, he did come back to the school, and managed to put his ego in check. Maybe it was just about maturing more. And once he did, my Kung Fu brother began to flourish in the system, and I couldn't have been happier for him.

> *Check your ego at the door. The ego can be the great success inhibitor. It can kill opportunities, and it can kill success.*
>> —Dwayne "The Rock" Johnson, athlete and actor

CLEARING THE DECKS, OR NOT

Judging others, being inflexible, and maintaining an attitude of superiority are qualities that will most likely impede your progress in both Kung Fu and life.

As a teacher, do your students come to you when they don't understand the lesson, or are they guarded about admitting they didn't get it the first time around? And if they are guarded over the simple need for a further explanation, is it due to *their* egos? Or have they interpreted past cues that *your* ego manifests itself in negative ways at that possible notion that your teaching wasn't up to par?

How about your children?

Your subordinates at work?

Ego is the Enemy

Perhaps you run the shipping department for your company, and everything moves in perfect harmony, with packages going out on time. You're so good at pulling things together that one of the executives decides to transfer you, putting you in charge of the receiving department, where things are a total mess. After two months with this new responsibility, receiving is moving forward but still not up to your personal standards. Then, at your company's year-end assessment meeting, one of the higher-ups praises the shipping department and their new leader, while making a point to downgrade receiving, and even mentioning your name. To make matters worse, the new leader of shipping accepts the praise without bringing up your previous influence.

Is this where you stand up and set the record straight? Or do you silently use this meeting as new motivation to work even harder at improving the receiving department?

Maybe you organized a community cleanup of your local beach, getting more than thirty volunteers to spend an entire morning collecting trash from along the shore. Two weeks later, at a meeting of community residents, you are presented with a shiny plaque for your organizational efforts, and are asked to say a few words. How willing are you to share praise? Do you thank the many people who showed up to participate in the cleaning? Do you elevate their efforts over yours?

At the time of his retirement, basketball icon Michael Jordan, who won a total of six NBA championships with the Chicago Bulls (a pair of three-peats, 1991 to 1993 and 1996 to 1998), was undoubtedly the most famous athlete in the world, and self-admittedly driven by a huge ego. But in his Hall of Fame induction speech in 2009, that ego, in part, took a back seat as MJ talked about how his parents and siblings were so important to his success.

"It all starts with my parents . . . They started the fire in me . . . and as I moved on in my career people added wood to that fire," said Jordan.

Sitting out in the large audience that night was someone special to the occasion, someone whom MJ had personally invited to the event, and even paid for their seat.

"Leroy Smith was the guy, when I got cut he made . . . the varsity team," said Jordan, who was forced to play another year on the JV squad at Emsley A. Laney High School in Wilmington, North Carolina. "He started the whole process for me. Because when he made the team and I didn't, I wanted to prove, not just to Leroy Smith and to myself, but to the coach who picked Leroy over me, to make sure that you understood you made a mistake."

German philosopher Friedrich Nietzsche believed that human beings crafted their own identity through self-realization. 'Whenever I climb, I am followed by a dog named 'Ego'" noted Nietzsche (1844–1900), who probably would have been Michael Jordan's biggest fan had they lived in the same time period.

NATURAL KUNG FU: DEFINING EGO

Dr. Kevin Kennedy, assistant chair of the philosophy department at St. John's University in New York, is uniquely interested in a branch of philosophy called metaphysics, which in part deals with the concepts of "being" and "identity." Naturally, those self-defining concepts are closely intertwined with ego.

"The good part about our ego is that it drives us to achieve things and accomplish our goals," noted Dr. Kennedy, who has authored several books on the broad subject of metaphysics. "But when the ego begins to get in our way, when we start comparing ourselves to others, either putting ourselves above or beneath them, instead of concentrating on the task at hand, it can become a problem in our lives."

Over his near forty-year tenure at St. John's, Dr. Kennedy witnessed many societal changes, including the birth of the internet, where egos can be bolstered or shattered via a single post.

"I discourage our instructors from reading their on-line student reviews [Rate My Professor]. Whenever we focus on things such as pleasing others, or where we stand in the pecking order, it can become counterproductive. It can take us out of 'the zone,' that place where we become one with the activity."

Dr. Kennedy is also the managing director of an award-winning Manhattan-based theatre company.

Did someone say actors and egos?

"Certainly there's ego in acting," observed Dr. Kennedy. "But actors who are worried about themselves instead of portraying their characters can really make a mess out of things. That's why I generally discourage actors from reading reviews of their performance, even a very positive review."

Why?

"Seeing described in print something that they might be doing well unconsciously can destabilize them and their process," said Dr. Kennedy.

PAUL'S PERSPECTIVE: SLY OLD FOX

Back in 2000, I wrote a short news article about a famous trainer of thoroughbred racehorses named P. G. Johnson, who had been an amazing caretaker of equines for six decades. Johnson enjoyed both the story and the translation of my last name, Volponi, which in Italian means *the sly old fox*. Because that's exactly what the trainer considered himself to be after such a long and storied career. Johnson actually named his next racehorse "Volponi."

I was thrilled and honored, especially after P. G. invited me and my family down to his barn to meet the spirited animal.

But whenever I was up in the racetrack's press box, I knew I'd have to keep a low profile about it, focusing on keeping any ego of mine about the naming in check. Why? Reporters are an interesting breed of their own. I knew that some of the writers there

[183]

would be pleased for me, while others would be annoyed about it, thinking I didn't deserve such a recognition.

The horse lost its first race. And I had to put my ego completely aside when some drunken fan in the grandstand, who had probably lost a few bucks by wagering, screamed at the colt, "Volponi, you suck!"

But things got more interesting when Volponi the horse actually started to win races.

Big, important races.

I was thrilled for P. G., who was nearing the end of his career. I'd show up in the paddock and shake his hand before every race in which Volponi was entered. And P. G. seemed to think I was a bit of good luck.

The more the horse won, the nastier the barbs got from a small band of ego-driven writers in the press box. *Volponi isn't that good. He's totally overrated.* I didn't want to vie my ego against theirs, though many times it was hard for me not to respond, either with words or envisioned blows.

A month later, P. G. wrote a sizable check to cover the late entry fee of Volponi into one of the world's biggest races, the $4 million Breeders' Cup Classic, which was being held in Chicago that year, where P. G. had started his career as a trainer.

Few believed that Volponi actually belonged in that race, and the comments grew sharper in describing what some perceived as a moronic pipe dream to even enter.

I wasn't in Chicago that day to cover the race, but that small band of ego-driven writers from the press box were, every one of them.

In the race, Volponi went off as a 43–1 longshot against the best horses in training, including War Emblem, who had won that year's Kentucky Derby.

I watched on TV from home with family and friends, yelling and screaming at the top of my lungs as Volponi pulled away

Ego is the Enemy

from the competition in the stretch. I displayed every ounce of ego possible as he crossed the finish line, considering that I didn't own, ride, or train the horse. He just had my name, which that weekend was splashed across the back page sports section of the several major New York newspapers.

That afternoon, Volponi banked $2.4 million in purse money for P. G. and his family. Not only did the colt win, he did it by the widest margin of victory any horse, up to that point, had in that esteemed contest.

A few days later, I walked back into the press box and didn't mention the victory to anyone. I remained meticulously silent, nodding hello to a select few and engaging in my work. I was there for probably fifteen minutes before someone approached me with congratulations, which I accepted. I then turned to one of the naysayer reporters seated to my left and politely thanked him for mentioning my name in his story.

If ego was truly the enemy, I signaled an understated truce that day, leaving others to talk about Volponi's triumph, and finding myself constantly trying to beat back what I'm sure was an ever-widening grin.

LIFE APPLICATIONS

- You have a chance at being the top individual bowler in your local league. But to achieve that goal, you need to bowl this Saturday, the same day as your niece's wedding. Do you miss the ceremony and attend the reception that night or do you sacrifice your chance at the honor and go to the wedding?
- Your best friend is in desperate need of a short-term loan. You know their pride would never allow them to ask you for money. So you write your friend a check without being asked.

- At every family gathering, your forty-five-year-old sibling brings up the fact that their score on the SAT was significantly higher than yours. And it has begun to bother you. Do you let it go, understanding that your sibling obviously has a need to feed their ego, or do you address it?
- Friends are watching as your dog won't listen to you, refusing to come on command. You feel yourself losing your temper. Ask yourself, *Would I be this upset if there was no one else here to witness the dog's refusal?*

Being a singer is all about me. About ego. Being a mom is all about being selfless—two different worlds.
—Gwen Stefani, musician

IMMENSE PRIDE
Bruce Lee took a tremendous amount of pride in his Kung Fu. So much so that when he received the script for a 1967 episode of *Batman*, the campy hit TV show of its time, he flew into a rage and stormed off from a studio where he was filming a TV series called *The Green Hornet*. At the time, Lee was playing the part of Kato, a man servant/butler to the main character, Britt Reid, aka the Green Hornet. The proposed script, in which the Green Hornet and Kato would be making a guest appearance on *Batman*, had Lee's character losing in a fight to Batman's sidekick, Robin. On the surface, it seemed semi-logical. After all, Batman and Robin were the stars of that show. However, Lee absolutely refused to take part, especially after rumors had circulated that the actor playing Robin, Burt Ward, who was a karate practitioner, allegedly told others around the studio that he was the real-life better fighter. Lee's

(continued next page)

Ego is the Enemy

co-star Van Williams, playing the Green Hornet, backed up his partner's stance, refusing to take part as well if the pair lost an on-screen fight to the Dynamic Duo.

In the end, the writers were forced to revamp the script. The aired episode entitled "A Piece of the Action" (Season 2, Episode 51), features the four protagonists getting into fisticuffs. The end result? They fought to a draw.

Though Bruce Lee played the role of a servant in *The Green Hornet*, he is widely recognized as a catalyst in changing the perceptions of Asians only playing subservient roles in western films, assuming leading-man status in vehicles such as *Enter the Dragon* (1973) and *Game of Death* (1978).

CHAPTER SEVENTEEN

RECOVERING FROM THE UNEXPECTED (*BIU JEE*)

No one is so brave that he is not disturbed by something unexpected.

—Julius Caesar

MY FATHER REFERRED TO the *Biu Jee* form as "Standard Compass," because no matter how hard you shake it or which way it gets turned around, it always returns to north. This is an attribute I'm sure you will want to transfer into your life as a way to right yourself after something unexpected tries to unduly influence your direction.

PHYSICAL ATTRIBUTES

Wing Chun's third open-hand form is called *Biu Jee*, which translates as *thrusting fingers*. There are credible reasons why your hands may momentarily leave the center line during an encounter, including the need to block a wide strike or deal with a surprise

Live Life Like a Kung Fu Master

attacker. The *Biu Jee* form focuses on the use of emergency techniques (*gow gup sau*) that conclude with a quick return to center. This can be accomplished by either quickly bringing your arm (or arms) back to center, or rotating your body to face your arms, creating a new center. In both cases, hitting or chopping at the center line speeds up this process by creating momentum, as well as presenting a formidable response.

Biu Jee builds on everything the practitioner has learned in both *Siu Nim Tao* and *Chum Kiu*. Why is *Biu Jee* necessary? Fighting can be a fluky endeavor filled with unexpected obstacles. When put into a compromising position, the Kung Fu practitioner can turn to the emergency techniques of *Biu Jee* in an effort to reestablish a more fundamental position. These emergency techniques, which include the thrusting of fingers, can quickly occupy the center for intercepting or deflecting incoming attacks.

Let's examine a pair of techniques from this third form, *biu sau* and elbow strikes.

A *biu sau* can either be used as an attack or block, led by the compressed fingers of a thrusting arm. It's normally used to address or create a situation at shoulder height or above, while being aimed at the eyes or throat.

The rotating elbow strikes (*gwai jaans*) in *Biu Jee* can be used as both an attack and a means of regaining center with the elbows reclaiming the center line, while traveling from either the left to right (or reverse). The elbow can also be paired with a following *biu sau* (emanating from beneath the armpit of the centered elbow) to further reestablish control of the center.

For a visual demonstration, go to YouTube and search: "Live Life Like a Kung Fu Master—William Moy, Demonstrating Biu Jee Form."

Recovering from the Unexpected (Biu Jee)

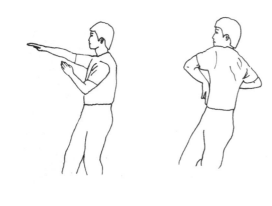

FROM MY LIFE: NO-WIN SUBWAY RIDE

I was in my late teens and traveling from Brooklyn to Chinatown in Manhattan to attend my father's Kung Fu class. The subway car in which I was riding was relatively empty. At one of the stops, several guys came bounding onto the train, laughing and joking with one another. It was a Saturday morning, so at first I thought they might have been members of a school sports team heading to a competition of some sort. But no. They were more like a group of junior gangbangers looking to test their strength in numbers.

It wasn't hard to spot their momentary leader, the one who was most likely the catalyst for their bad intentions. The other three were looking to him for directions as they checked out the surroundings—a lot of empty subway seats and me.

As the train rolled on between stations, their leader walked over to where I was sitting. At that moment, I could have been the Asian version of Peter Parker, aka Spider-Man, because all of my Kung Fu senses were tingling.

"Hey, do you belong to a gang?" their leader asked me.

I considered it a loaded question, and a no-win situation.

If I had answered yes, they might have perceived me as a rival and attacked. On the other hand, if I answered no, it would have

Live Life Like a Kung Fu Master

put me alone on an island, without the threat of added muscle to possibly even the score one day.

Maybe I should have asked to join their budding crew. Instead, I remarked that I didn't belong to a gang. The leader immediately demanded the leather jacket that I was wearing as a "tax" for riding the train through their turf.

I decided to stand my ground, and a fight ensued between me and their leader, with the other three wannabe gangbangers rushing over to join in.

Without hesitation, I grabbed their leader and tried to drive him into the wall of that moving subway car. It was a finishing move talked about by some of my Kung Fu brothers. Only things have a way of going down differently in real-world scenarios, and I wound up shoving him over a subway seat instead.

Then I got hit from behind by one of the other thugs, losing my center for a moment. But I immediately used the emergency techniques from *Biu Jee* to recover.

After a few more exchanges, I was able to escape through the opening doors when the train pulled into the next station.

When I finally arrived at the school, I informed my father about the fight. First and foremost, he was glad that I was uninjured. Then he slowly started to dissect my physical responses as I had described them. My father told me that I was rushing too much. That my attackers were also trapped on that train, and not going anywhere. He advised me that I should have put more of my horse into those punches, generating increased power, because my balance and ability to use the ground beneath me—especially on a moving train—probably far outweighed the abilities of my attackers in that area.

After pondering the situation, I realized that I should have been more adaptable to the free-flowing action, rather than being so focused on utilizing a specific technique.

[192]

Recovering from the Unexpected (Biu Jee)

And before I entered another subway car, I absolutely needed a better response to the question, *Hey, do you belong to a gang?*

> *Life inevitably throws us curve balls, unexpected circumstances that remind us to expect the unexpected.*
> —Carré Otis, model and actress

PREPPING WITH THE BASICS

Recovering from the unexpected is a quality of preparedness that Kung Fu can bring to your life. Every family as a whole should have a plan for what to do in an emergency. You don't have to live in an area where earthquakes, wildfires, tornadoes, or flash floods are always somewhere on the horizon. No one has the ability to either predict the future or safeguard their family from an isolated incident or natural disaster. It's not impossible for the fire department to knock on your door because of a neighborhood gas leak, instituting a mandatory evacuation of several blocks.

Having both a plan in place that details where your loved ones can go for shelter and exactly what you'll bring with you—either in a life-threatening emergency or during an inconvenient several-day stay out of your home—is simply smart planning. It's the same as knowing where the fire extinguishers are on every floor, making sure every member of your family can operate them, and that they are in working order.

Maybe you're surfing and an unexpected wave pitches you from the board, which then pops up and contacts your head just hard enough to stun you for a moment. Your first goal is to get back to the surface and take a deep breath. Then find your position in relation to the shore. You might call to other surfers for help, or perhaps a lifeguard already has eyes trained on the situation. And if you're still connected to the board via your ankle strap, you know that it can be used as a floatation device.

Live Life Like a Kung Fu Master

Suppose you're an adjunct professor at a local community college. You're teaching an introductory course to a large section of students. You know that your students are serious and well motivated. They participate in class giving you solid answers to the material in question, and their attendance is exemplary. You have high hopes for them as you administer their midterm exam. But nearly every student fails the exam you created, with many leaving answers totally blank. To whom does this unexpected outcome belong, you or the students? How can both the teacher and the class get past this disastrous result?

Mornings can often be hectic and stressful. Perhaps you awaken with a strict timetable staring you in the face. You need to print a proposal for work, but the printer is telling you that's it's offline. Your frustration starts to build and then spikes when your teary-eyed child informs you that they need to print something for school immediately. You've got one eye on the clock and need to be out the door with your child in tow in less than ten minutes. You check every connection multiple times, even getting down on the hardwood floor upon your sore knees to visually check the wiring. All seems lost until your significant other peeks their head out of the kitchen and suggests, "Just unplug the router and then restart everything."

In retrospect, that simple advice was a way of getting back to basics that somehow slipped your mind in the tense moment of the unexpected happening. And you know what? That suggestion worked.

NATURAL KUNG FU: COURAGE AND PATIENCE

Over his long tenure as a martial artist, Tish Das has studied a number of different arts with an intense focus on Kung Fu. The successful private wealth manager and his wife, Amisha, a PhD in epidemiology, are the proud parents of two healthy and beautiful

Recovering from the Unexpected (Biu Jee)

young children, and recently moved from New Jersey to the California coast where they purchased their dream home.

But life isn't always a totally smooth ride. Often the tides that swell can have designs on tossing about our mental and physical well-being.

Back in 1999, Tish was the recipient of a much-needed kidney transplant. The donor was his loving father, who has since sadly passed away. Today, Tish is in need of a second kidney transplant, awaiting his turn on a state list for an appropriate match.

"I view Kung Fu as a tool for relaxation, and engaging in the process of life. With it, I know that I can overcome any obstacle as my process continues to evolve. I can be the best version of myself at that moment, putting in the work to achieve that goal."

Several years ago, Das was surfing on the Jersey shore, riding a wave, when an adolescent suddenly moved into his oncoming path. "I changed course and rode the board up onto the shore. Then I jumped off, landing with both feet in the shallow whitewater. But I couldn't see the huge hole beneath the surface. That's when I heard the *pop*. And when you're in your forties, that's never a good sound."

The diagnosis was a ruptured right Achilles tendon. Das opted for rehab instead of surgery, and likened the experience to his years of training in Kung Fu. "You do the exercises over and over. It's about improving and getting better through small steps. It's always about engaging in the process. You need patience, courage, and the will to do it," noted Das, who is almost completely recovered.

Das credits a good portion of his patience to the example set for him by his sifu, William Moy. "Sifu is very steadfast. He never gets too high or too low. He's a great representation of the Kung Fu, totally embodying it. He's always in the moment, listening. That's what Kung Fu's about, learning how to listen to ourselves and others. It's provided a solid framework to my life."

Live Life Like a Kung Fu Master

LIFE APPLICATIONS

- You have a sudden flood in your basement, with water pouring in from a window ledge during a heavy rainstorm. Instead of running to the garage for a bucket, with water filling the basement in your absence, you begin using various accessible items such as an empty flowerpot, ice chest, and plastic storage container as makeshift buckets to catch the flood water, depositing it in a nearby slop sink.
- During a prolonged power outage, several neighbors ask you to hold perishable food items in your large pantry freezer because your home is the only one on the block with a backup generator.
- You encounter a senior walking down the street who seems disoriented. So you try to center their focus with questions such as, *Can you tell me your name? Where are you headed? On what street do you live?*
- While lost in the woods without a compass, someone in your party suggests to check the moss on the trees, which normally grows on the north side.

In life, there's a Yin and a Yang and a balance. And when you don't have balance, you have comedy.

—George Lopez, comedian

THE YIN AND YANG OF KUNG FU

One of the most recognizable symbols in the world today is that of the Yin and Yang teardrop circles, bringing together the superbly balanced black and white images. If you stopped most people on the street wearing the symbol as adornment upon their clothes, knapsack, or jewelry, the simple definition they might give you is that it represents "balance" and "harmony." And they would absolutely be correct, though its concepts can certainly be discussed on a much deeper plain, as they reflect upon subjects such as mathematics, Chinese medicine, and, of course, philosophy.

The dual concepts of Yin and Yang sprang from Chinese philosophy, representing two contrasting principles which couldn't singularly have meaning to us without the other as comparison. These principles include light/dark, positive/negative, hard/soft, and masculine/feminine. Together, they represented the concept of harmony in Chinese culture as early as the fourteenth century BCE.

So what's the connection between Yin (dark) and Yang (bright) and Kung Fu?

At this point, you've most likely learned enough about both the physical art of Kung Fu and its surrounding culture to answer this question for yourself,

(continued next page)

Live Life Like a Kung Fu Master

so feel free to do so before it's discussed in the next paragraph.

Because Kung Fu is considered both a soft (Yin) and hard (Yang) martial art, combining both power and contact reflexes to feel what's going on inside the opponent, it's a very strong representation of the Yin and Yang philosophy. In addition, Kung Fu is predicated on maintaining your balance while disrupting the balance of the opponent—again, two contrasting principles.

Finally, early on in this text we discussed people having "good Kung Fu" in life, a quality held in high regard in Chinese culture. For the concept of "good Kung Fu" to have meaning, it must be compared to those with less than that standard and, at times, the complete opposite.

How about the Yin and Yang symbol?

It is a Taoist symbol that first appeared in ancient Chinese time-keeping systems. Exactly *who* designed the symbol has remained a mystery through the ages. Unfortunate? Just imagine the copyright money they would be owed today.

Here is a trio of corresponding Wing Chun maxims to consider:

The Yin Yang principle should be thoroughly understood.

Beginners must not use strength.

Soft and relaxed strength will put your opponent in jeopardy.

CHAPTER EIGHTEEN

SIDESTEPPING POTENTIAL CONFLICT/ ACCEPTING THE UNAVOIDABLE

Man must evolve for all human conflict a method which rejects revenge, aggression and retaliation.
—Dr. Martin Luther King Jr.

KUNG FU, AND ESPECIALLY Wing Chun, is designed to help you avoid conflicts in your life. To be clear, in the correct circumstance you'll step directly into the fray and face conflict head-on. But that choice will always be yours. Once you truly acquire and refine your Kung Fu, you won't be goaded into unwanted conflict.

PHYSICAL ATTRIBUTES

Wing Chun teaches you to martial distance early during an unfolding encounter, and to never willing surrender your critical distance (your "safety zone"). But in doing so, this means that you'll extend your arms (perhaps in an obvious *jong sau*, or

Live Life Like a Kung Fu Master

something less visually provocative) with your hands lined up one behind the other and your elbows protecting your body. You'll use your voice to dissuade and discourage potential opponents from advancing—*Stop! Stop there! Stay back!* You might even appease them with your words. *You're right! I'm sorry!* If it's safe to do so, you'll walk away from trouble. You might even run when prudent. But that's far different from being bullied, something your Kung Fu will never allow.

Just because you have a strong desire to sidestep potential conflict whenever possible, that doesn't mean that you won't throw the first strike or execute the initial kick in an encounter once your critical distance is encroached. Despite your best efforts, some encounters will be unavoidable and beyond your control to prevent.

FROM MY LIFE: THREE PHASES OF CONFLICT/ ACCEPTANCE

Learning

As a young Kung Fu player, I experienced conflict. At first, I perceived that conflict to be with my training partner during rounds of *chi sau* to see who could control the center and land the most techniques. Whenever I was dominated at such a task, which was often in the beginning, I would grow severely frustrated with my lack of ability. That began to change the conflict I felt, projecting it fully onto myself. Filled with a growing self-doubt, I decided to take a break from *chi sau* for several weeks.

After processing my feelings under my father's guidance, I returned to the exercise with a new perspective on my struggles. I decided to adopt the philosophical concept similar to "Leaves on the Stream," accepting the direction and results in which the exercise led me. I became the observer, interpreting any misplays on my part as a learning experience that would eventually result in my ability to improve. Once the tenseness created by the potential of conflict left my body, I was able to relax. I accepted the unavoidable: that I was not a perfect player, and that I would make mistakes.

In my new state of being, I was capable of feeling and listening better with my hands, translating my partner's intentions—often just in the infancy of them happening. My *chi sau* play was on the road to improving, and so was my overall grasp of Kung Fu.

Teaching

As a beginning sifu, I took great pride in guiding students through our Wing Chun system, and celebrating their achievements. But every so often, a bright and talented student would simply miss a concept completely and be unable to successfully perform a technique, while their classmates almost instantly took to it. I could sense the conflict building inside of that lone student. Just starting out in my profession, I could sense the frustration in myself as well, feeling that perhaps it was about my shortcomings as a teacher and communicator. For the most part, the shaken student would simply try harder and harder, developing a sort of tunnel vision in that moment, virtually blocking out any directional input.

Eventually, I learned to explain to such students, who could be anyone anywhere at a particular instant trying to master something new, the importance of briefly detaching oneself from the task at hand. The goal is to achieve joy in the learning process. Relax, breathe, and let time and practice dictate your progress, not the moment.

It was a valuable lesson that I learned for myself, too. And I'm pleased to say that most of my students who have faced such a budding conflict now look back at that difficult to learn technique as a stepping stone in their own Kung Fu maturation process.

Live Life Like a Kung Fu Master

Working

I was just a few days into a new job when I was left to hold down the fort alone while the business owner was at home dealing with some personal matters. It had been a rather hectic day, as I wore several different hats to address arising issues. An hour before closing, a contractor came in and dropped off an agreement concerning some upcoming construction. He insisted that it had to be signed immediately. I took him seriously and said that I would drop it off at the boss's house personally on my way home from work. Over the next hour, three separate issues arose that needed immediate attention, taking up my focus.

More than four hours later, I found myself at home with my family, having already eaten dinner and halfway through a TV whodunit mystery when I suddenly remembered the contract. After some internal debate about the hour possibly being too late, I called the boss and told him how I screwed up, forgetting to deliver the contract. I just wanted to face any potential conflict over my mistake while it was still in its infancy, and not something full blown. I even offered to get dressed and drive it over at that moment.

He told me to relax, that contractors were always making up stories to get contracts signed right away. And then he thanked me for diligently looking after his interests.

It was a valuable lesson for me on business speak, and how one party's supposed emergency/conflict might in fact be nothing more than impatience.

> *I'm just trying like everybody else. I try to take every conflict, every experience, and learn from it.*
> —Oprah Winfrey, media personality

Sidestepping Potential Conflict/Accepting the Unavoidable

THE PARKING CONFLICT

Perhaps you and your next-door neighbors have a different idea of exactly how to share your connecting driveway. The driveway is on the narrow side to begin with, and your neighbors own a huge four-wheel-drive SUV. It would be extremely tight with their vehicle parked adjacent to yours, a compact car, under normal conditions. But your neighbors always take an extra foot of room, parking onto your side of the driveway. That leaves your car routinely nestled against a rose bush, taking the absolute worst of the auto-meets-flora union.

Your neighbors are incredibly nice about the situation, blaming themselves for their poor parking. They apologize profusely to you twice a week. But nothing in the unbalanced driveway equation changes.

How can you affect a change in your neighbors' parking behavior?

After meeting with them, both parties decide on a set of three orange traffic cones. When your neighbors pull out of the driveway, someone will get out of their SUV and place the cones horizontally across their half of the driveway. This way they'll be focused on the situation when they return. It works great on day one. Not a problem. But on day two, their vehicle is gone and the cones aren't set out.

Since you're progressing so rapidly in your study of this art, we'll ask you: What might be the next step in employing your good Kung Fu to address the quandary?

NATURAL KUNG FU: CONFLICT RESOLUTION

Can personal, professional, and social conflict actually be good for us to experience? Professor Michelle LeBaron, who is a conflict transformation scholar/practitioner at the University of British Columbia in Canada, believes that it can be essential to our growth as individuals.

Live Life Like a Kung Fu Master

"Conflict can be an engine for social change and teach us many things about ourselves and others," said Professor LeBaron. "But what we really need to do is learn how to be in conflict well, respecting the opinions of others. People have been in conflict since the dawn of time and we're still here. There's even a Chinese character that stands for both conflict-crisis and opportunity."

The two ideas also share a Chinese proverb which states the following: A crisis is an opportunity riding a dangerous wind.

Can two untrained parties truly resolve their conflicts without the help of a trained mediator?

"Well, it all depends on who the parties are," said Professor LeBaron. "Will they really listen to one another, talk and act sincerely? Try to understand the other's point of view? Can they still their own needs for a time? Transforming conflict can be very difficult. You absolutely need to pay attention to the process."

Much of the conflict in our world tends to be either cultural or generational, and sometimes a mix of both. Consider someone from the East and someone from the West with different principles working side by side for eight hours a day. A conservative mindset versus a liberal mindset in the same carpool five days a week. A teenager and a parent with dissimilar views on what it means to be an adult trying to establish a curfew. All of these have the potential for creating major conflicts.

Is resolving conflicts best achieved through a face-to-face meeting?

"For the most part it's better that way, but not always. Consider the animal kingdom and two dogs looking each other in the eye. There's always a chance for an escalation," said Professor LeBaron. "It's better that people are in the same room, or at least communicating over Zoom. You can pick up a lot of cues when you can see the other person. It's often better that they sit at angles to one another, and have more of a soft gaze. Consider that couples often solve problems on long walks, when they're both present in the moment, but not actually face to face."

[204]

Sidestepping Potential Conflict/Accepting the Unavoidable

Bridging is a term in both Kung Fu and conflict resolution, with close to the same meaning, feeling what the other side is expressing.

"In conflict bridging, it's usually the mediator who gets stepped on by both sides, actually providing each party with some common ground."

Is it possible that those with martial arts experience could conceivably have a few more tools to quash potential conflicts?

"I think so because many martial arts focus on the principle of giving a little bit before you respond," noted Professor LeBaron.

PAUL'S PERSPECTIVE: STEPPING FORWARD

My wife April occasionally enters the daily lottery to win reduced-priced tickets to Broadway shows. After being notified she'd won for a particular show, we unexpectedly found ourselves driving into Manhattan from Queens in the early evening, parking and then walking to the theater.

Even though it was a weeknight, the sidewalks of Times Square were filled with tourists, theater goers, and an assortment of native New Yorkers like us. Whenever I'm walking through the crowded streets of Manhattan, my antenna is always up, keeping a careful lookout for those with either personal problems or less-than-honorable intentions.

While April was preoccupied with the brilliant signage and sparkling lights, my ears picked up an interesting sound. It was the stereotypical sound made by a combatant in a cheesy Kung Fu movie, a high-pitched *high-yah*.

I glanced over my shoulder and spotted a tall man, probably in his late twenties, wearing a ragged T-shirt and walking with an exaggerated bounce to his step. He gave me the immediate impression of someone having a hard time handling his emotions.

He stepped directly into the path of an older woman, most likely in her fifties, making that noise again, and picking his

Live Life Like a Kung Fu Master

hands up to her. His hands turned in a sideways circle, just like theatrical-based Kung Fu. The woman let out small *gasp*, probably too frightened to scream, until several people she was with ushered her in the opposite direction, away from potential harm.

April had completely missed that interaction, but I subtly brought us to a halt, wanting to secure a safer space as I watched that young man continue past us.

I felt sorry for him, and from working with so many troubled adolescents over my years in education understood that he didn't have complete control over his actions. I let him get a good ways ahead of us into the dense crowd before we started to walk again.

Because he was so tall, I could see his head bobbing overtop of everyone else's. As the fates would have it, the young man seemingly turned on a dime, heading back in our direction. His eyes locked on to mine as he started to steam straight toward me.

The fake Kung Fu guy was about to try a student of the art.

If there were a path around him on that crowded street, I would have taken it. But there wasn't. He stopped approximately five feet from me, directly on my center line. As he started to spin his hands in a circle again, I immediately went into *jong sau* and significantly closed the gap between us to jam him up.

My hands knifed through his, and my fingertips contacted his chin. He immediately jumped back several feet. If I were geared for a real fight, I would have followed after him, giving him no quarter.

But I didn't. I never wanted to hurt him.

I just needed him out of my space for both our protection.

The young man angrily stalked off down the street, with the crowd moving out of his way. He got maybe a hundred feet from where I still stood before he turned to a metal sandwich sign on the sidewalk and punched it with all of his might.

I don't know how he didn't break his hand.

He turned the first corner, disappearing into the crowd.

Sidestepping Potential Conflict/Accepting the Unavoidable

April was upset and a little shaken.

"Do you still want to see this show? Can you really sit through a performance and enjoy it after that?" she asked in a concerned voice.

"Sure. Everything's fine and nobody got hurt," I said. "I just hope that guy gets some help."

Five minutes later, at the door to the theater, she asked, "How can you be so calm and just file away what happened?"

The straightforward answer came to me rather easily.

"That's what you can do when you train," I said. "I didn't take it personally. It wasn't about me. It was about *him*. That's what having a little Kung Fu will do for you, help you to see situations more clearly and respond. Let's go into the show."

LIFE APPLICATIONS

- A checkout counter clerk insists that your discount coupon for groceries has expired, even though there's no expiration date printed on it. You argue your side of the facts, but the conversation quickly comes to an impasse, with the clerk becoming somewhat surly. That's when you end the back and forth, asking for the manager.

- You receive a sweater as a birthday present from your aunt. The style is definitely not you. It's also a tad tight around the shoulders, so you let her know that you love her present, but the size is too small. She gives you the sales receipt and you exchange it for a sweater in a style more to your liking . . . and one in the proper size.

- Someone is smoking in a non-smoking area and it's causing your asthma to flare. Instead of getting in an exchange with the rule breaker, you simply inform security and let them handle it.

- Another couple wants to split the dinner check. Only they've had two appetizers, dessert, and a glass of wine each, while you and your significant other simply had an entrée. They've done this before. This time you were prepared, and surreptitiously prearranged for the server to bring two separate checks, avoiding a potential conflict and hard feelings.

Peace is not absence of conflict, it is the ability to handle conflict by peaceful means.
—Ronald Reagan, former US President

HONORED GUEST: DOC-FAI WONG (SAN FRANCISCO/GUANGDONG PROVINCE, CHINA)
Grandmaster Doc-Fai Wong has been teaching the art of Kung Fu for more than a half-century. He specializes in Choy Li Fut, a blending of animal-inspired forms and powerful hand techniques found in Southern Chinese Kung Fu, along with the agile footwork and body movements represented in the styles of the North.

"As a little kid in my hometown (Wangshan village of the Guangdong province), my family took me to see the Cantonese Opera. The scenes that displayed martial arts, with weapons and swords, captured my imagination," said Grandmaster Wong. "When I arrived in San Francisco as a young teen, I was easily spotted as an F.O.B. (Fresh off the Boat arrival), and that constantly made me a target of bullies. So I got scared and wanted to learn how to defend myself."

The youngster's desire to learn was strong, and he sought out the knowledge of those with experience.

"Whenever I saw somebody who knew martial arts, I would ask them to teach me. Then, when I lived in

(continued next page)

Sidestepping Potential Conflict/Accepting the Unavoidable

San Francisco's Chinatown, next to the big theater (Great Star Theater, which hosted Chinese operas, movies and entertainment), I finally found a school.

Wong learned Choy Li Fut from Lau Bun, who was among the very first to bring the art to the US, from the time they met in the early 1960s until Lau Bun's passing in 1967.

"Back then, at tournaments, Kung Fu representatives only did forms. There was no fighting. But I saw other participants warming up to spar, so I followed them."

Wong made such an impact with his art by attacking his opponents' limbs that many observers and friends wanted to learn from him. Soon he opened up his first school at the age of nineteen, teaching out of a garage.

"Kung Fu was experiencing great popularity during the early 1970s, because of the TV series *Kung Fu*, with David Carradine, and the films of Bruce Lee. So my number of students grew," noted Grandmaster Wong.

Wanting to learn more about his art, including some of the forgotten forms, Wong pursued the roots of Choy Li Fut on a trip to China, where he was serendipitously seated next to Master Hu Yuen Chu at a martial arts dinner. The next day, the pair practiced together. Even at an advanced age, Chu, displaying his incredible martial prowess, launched Wong several feet in the opposite direction and over a small balcony to the tier below. That impressed Wong, and thus began a long student-teacher discipleship between them.

Grandmaster Wong also recalled the downturn in Kung Fu's popularity during the succeeding decades. "People would call the school wanting to learn karate. Disappointed in my answer, they would hang up."

Today, in his mid-seventies, the Grandmaster's beloved art of Choy Li Fut and his worldwide schools are thriving.

(continued next page)

Live Life Like a Kung Fu Master

"Now, people ask me, 'Do you teach Kung Fu?' And often I reply, 'Why, do *you* like Kung Fu?' I've come to realize that it's not my job to explain Kung Fu, but to get you to my school so that you can experience it for yourself."

CHAPTER NINETEEN

The Wooden Dummy and Beyond

The expectations of life depend upon diligence; the mechanic that would perfect his work must first sharpen his tools.

—Confucius

EVEN IF YOU HAD never heard of Wing Chun Kung Fu, you would probably be familiar with the vision of one of its main training tools: the *Muk Yan Jong*, or, as it is more commonly called, the wooden dummy. You may have seen actors and martial artists such as Jackie Chan and Donnie Yen train on one with blinding speed and precision. And why not? It makes for amazing entertainment. Learning the wooden dummy form, though, is no small feat, and the dedication it takes simply to arrive at that starting point will influence corresponding avenues of your daily life in wholly positive ways.

Live Life Like a Kung Fu Master

PHYSICAL ATTRIBUTES

The wooden dummy is a vital step in perfecting a Kung Fu practitioner's positioning and footwork, as well as developing economical transitions from one position to another. The form associated with the dummy, consisting of 108 separate moves, is the fourth form in the Wing Chun system. Legend subscribes that the form comes from the Shaolin Temple, where a gauntlet of 108 dummies stood, which each used to perfect a singular move or technique.

Traditionally, wooden dummies in Mainland China were anchored in the ground (*day jong*). But after relocating to Hong Kong, which had mostly concrete floors, Ip Man approached a carpenter friend named Jo Muk Hin to change the dummy's design. In 1951, Hin presented Ip Man with a prototype of a dummy suspended on thin wooden slats running through the main trunk, attached to a portable frame. As an unexpected bonus, the horizontal slats flexed when a practitioner contacted the trunk, giving the dummy a spring-like action and mimicking the energy an opponent might send back. Though to be absolutely clear, a wooden dummy cannot replace a human partner or replicate one's actions. It is merely a substitute.

My father often stressed to students who reached the stage of the wooden dummy form in their training, "It's the same as a typewriter. You can't learn from a typewriter. But you can use the typewriter to do a better job for writing."

The dummy has three arms and one leg. The arms are not meant to be physical representations of an actual opponent's appendages. Rather, they represent the positioning of your opponent's attack and pathways of potential energy. Because the dummy doesn't actually change position (moving forward, backward, or to either side, as an opponent might upon absorbing your energy), the practitioner doing the form readjusts their body position several times to compensate for the tool's stationary nature.

[212]

The Wooden Dummy and Beyond

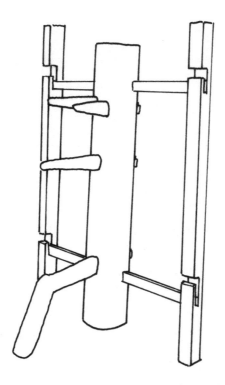

For a visual demonstration, go to YouTube and search: "Live Life Like a Kung Fu Master—William Moy, Demonstrating Wooden Dummy Form."

FROM MY LIFE: THAT SINGULAR SOUND

I recall practicing on the wooden dummy as a teen after class in my father's Chinatown school, with my father doing artwork in the back studio. I was aware that any excessive noise from the dummy might draw his disapproval. Not that it would break his concentration on a watercolor canvas, but because he could listen to the sound and know if it were being done correctly . . . or not. Hitting the dummy's arms too hard could lead you to overshoot your intended position when the same energy were to be transferred onto a real-life self-defense scenario. He would also listen for the near singular sound of multiple arms being hit at once with the correct timing, especially during techniques such as *gong sau* (cultivating hand used to block mid-low-level attacks) and *kwan sau* (rotating hand used to block high and low attacks simultaneously).

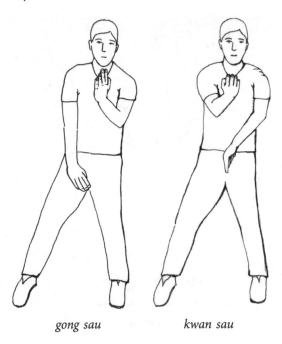

gong sau   kwan sau

My father taught me to randomly remove one of the dummy's three arms and then check to see if my applied technique landed in the precise location where the arm had rested. Taking that premise one step further, he also taught me to play the form in the air without a dummy, referred to as *Dar Hung Jong*, the empty Jong form. This exercise can really boost your overall precision, teaching you not to overshoot, because there is nothing there to absorb your energy.

There's a reason that a simplistic looking tool like the wooden dummy, or *jong*, is Wing Chun's fourth form. You need to learn all of the techniques and their possible combinations,

The Wooden Dummy and Beyond

both hands and legs, to attempt it. Newbies are often fascinated by the dummy, watching their older Kung Fu brothers and sisters play its form. Many experienced practitioners, however, consider a beginning student walking over to the dummy and throwing a few strikes at its limbs to be like a first-time driver being haphazardly put behind the wheel of a Ferrari on a Grand Prix racetrack. There's just a knowledge and experience that's glaringly absent.

> *One of the greatest and simplest tools for learning more and growing is doing more.*
> —Washington Irving, writer and historian

NATURAL KUNG FU: THE WOODEN HORSE

Champion thoroughbred jockey Frank Lovato Jr. showed a good bit of Kung Fu by designing something remarkably similar to Wing Chun's wooden dummy. At the age of eighteen, back in late 1981, Lovato suffered a broken leg on the racetrack and needed some sort of training device to help him regain his best riding form. He imagined something that could mimic the positions of race riding, much in the way the wooden dummy allows a solo Kung Fu practitioner to train various techniques.

"At the time, I was doing a lot of rehab and physical therapy, but I wasn't getting the flexibility that I needed in my knee to assume a riding position and properly straddle a horse. Then, after a second surgery, the knee began to get even stiffer," recalled Lovato. "I remembered when I was a little kid, I desperately wanted to ride, but didn't have my own horse. So I went by a local construction site, took some discarded scraps of wood, and built myself one."

That childhood memory inspired Lovato who, with the help of a handy friend, invented the first prototype of what is known

Live Life Like a Kung Fu Master

worldwide today as the Equicizer, a spring-loaded facsimile of a thoroughbred that enables people to either learn how to ride or polish their skills in the saddle.

"It was an amazing success for me," said Lovato, who eventually made a triumphant return to the racetrack. "Years later, the Equicizer was used in *Seabiscuit* (2003). The film's star, Tobey Maguire, wasn't a rider. So he trained exclusively on it to get the feel of being on a horse. In all the scenes where they're going faster than a gallop, the Equicizer was used. It was put onto a flatbed trailer and a thoroughbred's head was superimposed (also with help from a prosthetic) over the device's wooden one. Even the real jockeys in the film rode them. The controlled circumstances helped the camera to better capture their facial expressions as they were supposedly riding."

Today, with the help of several part-time workers, Frank Lovato makes about seventy Equicizers a year by hand, and his ingenious creation has aided both novice and professional riders everywhere.

WEAPONS TRAINING

The Wing Chun Kung Fu system also contains a pair of weapons forms: the Six and a Half Point Pole (*Luk Dim Boon Kwan*), often referred to as the Mouse Tail Pole (due to its tapering end), and the Butterfly Knives (*Baat Jaam Do*). And though you'll almost certainly never be in a battle with these two weapons against a similarly armed attacker, training with them both will absolutely improve your Kung Fu skills.

The form for each weapon is normally taught at the conclusion of the system as acquired by practitioners, and are an extension of many skills previously learned and refined over years of diligent training.

For example, learning the pole reinforces a low horse stance, sinking your body weight and strong rooting to the ground. It can also improve a practitioner's power by focusing on the body as a fulcrum to manipulate the weight of the pole (weighing approximately five pounds), as well as strengthening the wrists.

The Double Knives (one in each hand) are equal to the average length of a practitioner's forearm and fist combined. Learning this form helps to further define the concept of coverage, not to trade blows with an attacker (since you wouldn't want to absorb a strike from a blade), but to develop power through the core and waist, and intensify your focus on the tip of the blade the same way we focus our power to the end of an open-handed (weaponless) strike.

Live Life Like a Kung Fu Master

For a visual demonstration, go to YouTube and search: "Live Life Like a Kung Fu Master—William Moy, Introducing Pole and Double Knives."

PAUL'S PERSPECTIVE: SEATED

I was in love with the feel of the wooden dummy at Sifu William's school in Bayside, Queens. It was the dummy on which I originally learned the form. That dummy had a remarkably natural feel to it. I could close my eyes while training on it and almost believe that I was receiving feedback from a human partner. So when I eventually got a dummy of my own, mounted upon the frame of my basement stairs, the feel wasn't exactly the same, and I was always just a bit disappointed at that.

As a sportswriter working out of a press box, I came to realize that most writers, seated for a good portion of the day, were hugely possessive of their chairs, believing that no other chair there had the same feel to it. And I've witnessed several shouting matches and near blows over possession of a favorite chair.

It didn't really matter to me, as I'd sit in any chair available. They basically all looked the same. And, in my opinion, the difference in feel between them was barely noticeable.

One day, one of the writers stood up and made an insulting speech. He proclaimed himself an *everyday writer*, meaning he was there five days a week, and therefore much more entitled to a preferred chair than the *weekend people*, like myself, who mostly worked just Saturday and Sunday. His anger-filled remarks were so over the top that I didn't challenge them at the time, believing it could have led to a nasty encounter between us.

When I returned early the next morning to work on a story, I was the first one to arrive at the press box. I noticed that same incredulous writer had put a four inch long piece of scotch tape running vertically down the back of his chair as a marker to

[218]

recognize it. I knew that it wouldn't be right for me to remove the tape. There is a trust between writers never to mess with each other's property in the press box, though the chair did belong to the racetrack and not him.

Instead, I measured out six other four-inch pieces of scotch tape, putting them in the exact same place on the backs of different chairs. Then I moved those chairs over to his, and mixed them up, my own mischievous take on the game of musical chairs.

Lo and behold, five minutes after I had finished, this same writer was the next to arrive. I quietly sat ten feet away from his desk, on a chair with no tape, working at my laptop, but also watching him. He saw the tape on all of those chairs and looked totally perplexed. One by one, he put his behind down into each, trying to figure out which was actually his.

He had to have known it was me who taped all of those chairs, but he chose to never address it. Maybe he just didn't want to give me any more satisfaction than I was already feeling. Eventually, he sat himself down and went to work in the wrong chair.

Watching him struggle with those chairs actually cured me of my disfavor with the wooden dummy hanging in my basement. And from that day on, I began to cherish the feel of my own dummy and stopped wishing to be training on any other.

LIFE APPLICATIONS

- You take it upon yourself to hang multiple posters on several office walls by eye, without the correct tools. That's when one of your coworkers says that some of the posters are ever so slightly tilted to the right or left. So you approach your company's maintenance department in search of a level.

Live Life Like a Kung Fu Master

- Your child has become focused on gaining acceptance to a high school calculus class. So you ask for a conference with their math teacher, who says your child simply isn't ready because they haven't passed Algebra 2 yet.
- Unable to find a partner to practice dancing on your schedule, you begin to concentrate on dances that you can practice alone.
- Though you'll probably never be challenged to a fencing duel on the street, you enjoy training at the sport, knowing it brings a lot of positives to your life.

We become what we behold. We shape our tools and then our tools shape us.
—Marshall McLuhan, philosopher and media critic

CHAPTER TWENTY

TAKING YOUR *GOOD KUNG FU* INTO TOMORROW

I exhort you also to take part in the great combat,
which is the combat of life, and greater than every other
earthly conflict.

—Plato

IT'S DIFFICULT FOR ME to explain just how grateful I am. I'm grateful for my parents and family, and especially for my father, Moy Yat, who passed down to me this great system of Wing Chun Kung Fu with which I've been able to influence the lives of my students. And since you've made it this far into our book, perhaps you truly will think of me as your sifu, your guide in the art of Kung Fu.

Throughout these many pages, it has never been my intention to teach you how to fight, something that would be incredibly difficult to learn by simply reading a book. Rather, it has been my intention to teach you how to defend yourself and your loved ones in many common situations—on the street, at home, school,

[221]

and in the workplace—mostly through your choice of words, your ability to anticipate and thereby prepare for events, and your ability to choose a path leading to non-violent action.

I suppose some martial arts measure effectiveness by the number of altercations their students win. In my mind, I like to think about it differently. You see, I would much rather celebrate the number of altercations my students successfully avoid.

But if you do find yourself faced with the unavoidable, remember the concepts you've learned herein. Martial your space through distance awareness, allowing no one whom you do not fully trust into your critical distance. Fill your center line with *jong sau*, both arms extended with one hand lined up behind the other and your elbows protecting your body. Understand that it's alright to say, "Leave me alone," "Please go away," and even "Don't hurt me." Your raised voice combined with your posture will convey that you are not afraid.

Always maintain your facing (*doi ying*), and never look away from a potential threat. Your eyes and your attention to detail, while keeping the emerging threat squarely on your center line, will naturally bolster your abilities. Keeping proper facing will also help you to maintain good balance. Sink your body weight, grip the ground with your feet, and remember to move as a singular unit.

If you have your critical distance secured, the center line filled, your facing and your balance, then you can be confident and relaxed in your ability to successfully defend yourself.

THE IMPACT ON YOUR LIFE

Many martial artists train diligently for years and never have to use their skills in a physical encounter. I sincerely hope that you will be able to count yourself among them. So then, what would be the payoff for all of your hard work, if not winning a fight?

Taking Your Good Kung Fu *into Tomorrow*

As we've experienced, Wing Chun Kung Fu is a very adaptable art, making it extremely accessible for personal growth and overall improvement in varied aspects of daily living. Consider one of the system's maxims: *The theory of Wing Chun has no limit in it applications.* It doesn't matter if you're riding in a carpool, waiting in line at the checkout counter, or making your way to an open seat in a darkened theatre, your Kung Fu will always be in your back pocket.

The art's Center Line Theory teaches us to be straight and direct with others and ourselves. By traveling the shortest distance between two points, both literally and figuratively, it enables us to save precious time and have less wasted effort. We also learned about the value of structure and positioning. That when we fail to be in possession of either of these attributes, whether we're creating a professional report for our job or trying to negotiate a narrow staircase with a basket full of laundry, the outcome may be less than satisfactory.

The concept of redirecting external forces shows us how we can diminish outside pressures that may be hoisted upon us in many different scenarios, from work to social engagements. In subduing those pressures, the idea of being relaxed allows us to bend and not break; being tense simply gives opposing force a firm handle on our body to move us, mentally and physically, in the direction it desires us to go. And the training exercise of *chi sau* gives us a blueprint on how to combine many abilities at once: balance, structure, facing, relaxation, holding center, and keeping both hands alive while they're working independently from each other. It is an exercise that proves to us that we can indeed become masters of multitasking.

YOUR GOOD KUNG FU

As discussed in our introduction, the idea of possessing good Kung Fu goes well beyond the practitioner's ability to fight.

Live Life Like a Kung Fu Master

Chinese culture actually places a higher value on people who treat others respectfully while having control of their own lives. That's my fondest hope for all of my students, including you: for someone to observe your actions and say that you possess "good Kung Fu."

Sometimes you see it in very simple things.

I recall being at a delightful gathering of friends and family at a local restaurant. Everyone seemed to be extraordinarily hungry, awaiting the arrival of a piping-hot clay pot filled with a delicious beef stew. As the waiter set the dish down before my father, everyone's anticipation heightened. Seizing the opportunity to make the meal more accessible for everyone, my father deftly grabbed the pot by its handles and smoothly lifted it toward the Lazy Susan in the center of the table. Somehow naturally in sync with his actions, I swiftly slid a cork coaster beneath the pot to stop it from scorching the glass turntable. This seamless yet unplanned coordination tickled several in attendance, and someone said, "Now that was good Kung Fu."

How did we manage such a feat without verbal clues or gestures?

While sitting at that table, I was completely present, watching the actions of both the waiter and my father. Once my father grabbed the pot's handles, I understood what his intent would be and acted accordingly, using common sense and logic.

For me, on a daily basis, having good Kung Fu is about being present in the moment. And, of course, I'm borrowing that concept from Zen Buddhism. As Buddha once said, "The past is already gone, the future is not here yet. There's only one moment for you to live, and that is the present moment."

Keep attuned to the present and your good Kung Fu will be exemplary.

Taking Your Good Kung Fu *into Tomorrow*

> *Perfection is not attainable, but if we chase perfection we can catch excellence.*
> —Vince Lombardi, Hall of Fame football coach

PAUL'S PERSPECTIVE: UPON STUDYING

Kung Fu practitioners are a lot like urban gardeners. You might see someone walking down a crowded city street carrying a trowel and hoe. Then you begin to think to yourself, *I wonder where they're going with those things in the midst of all of this concrete?* Our fast-paced society often offers us little time to both appreciate and experience the natural process of growth. The hurried lure of the next impending moment, which might fulfill dreams of making you a millionaire, pop star, or viral internet sensation on any one of a dozen platforms, is where many of us spend our focus. Martial artists, however, have a tendency to take their time a bit more. They are mostly in no hurry for success. Instead, they patiently turn the soil, plant seeds, water, fertilize, and, eventually, reap the harvest of what they've sown through studying in class.

The hope is that the fruits of this enlightened harvest will be continual, lasting a lifetime. That the nourishment provided will also feed others who find themselves in our orbit, even total strangers. For the sharing of good Kung Fu is as easy as bumping into someone and hearing an *excuse me*, instead of *you should have gotten out of my way.* So if you see someone riding the bus or subway wearing gardening gloves, recognize that they might one day be responsible for a brilliant yellow sunflower sprouting up right outside of your apartment building, on that seemingly forgotten patch of brown earth. And that possibility is truly something to be applauded.

Live Life Like a Kung Fu Master

LIFE APPLICATIONS

- When faced with a disappointing result of a task at which you thought you'd succeed, you look back at your preparation in an attempt to see where you might improve on your foundational skills.
- In shaking hands with someone you're about to interview for a position with your company, you can actually feel the tenseness that they're experiencing through their grip. So you decide on leading a quick tour of your building, introducing that interviewee to several employees in an effort to make them feel more at ease.
- A pair of neighbors are in the midst of an argument just outside your front door. You realize that they're about to verbally take the disagreement to the next level, possibly saying things that can never be taken back. So you intervene vocally, making yourself the focus and interrupting their efforts by unbalancing the flow of their argument.
- You're sitting in the stands for your child's soccer game. This week, however, you decide to leave your cell phone in the car as to not be distracted from the real-time scene in front of you.

The ideal in martial arts is humanitarianism. Accomplishment uses diligence as a goal.

—Ip Man

Departing Thoughts

ON CAR RIDES

Car rides often provide the opportunity to spend some quality private time with those who are traveling together. That's the way it was for my father and me driving back home from Kung Fu class together, mostly with him behind the wheel and me in the front passenger seat. With the onrushing world shut out behind the windshield, those car rides gave us time alone to talk, openly and honestly.

No other family members.

No students from class vying for my father's attention.

Just the two of us.

One particular talk that we shared remains exceptionally close to my heart. I was a teen experiencing difficulty with my schoolwork and choosing a possible direction for a future career. It all weighed so heavily upon me that I actually missed out on time training, as I was unable to properly focus.

At the time, my father had been patiently carving and polishing a piece of jade for an art project. He told me about all the difficulties he faced in doing so, how each cut of the jade felt like it meant so much to the end result that it needed to be perfect. And how any potential misstep along the way gave the impression that it would completely ruin the project.

He went on to tell me that those fears and apprehensions concerning the jade were actually meaningless. That the artist's eye would eventually bring added beauty to the shimmering stone, no matter the route taken.

"A grindstone can either wear a stone down or polish it brightly. It's all about the artist who holds it in their hands," my father said. "It's about how that person views the world."

It was a simple analogy, but one that had a great impact upon me at exactly the right moment.

By the time I stepped out of that car, I realized that the power to give direction to my life was in my own hands. My intense malaise had begun to fade behind the renewed faith I found in myself, the faith that I could eventually make the right road out of any choice.

And for you, my readers: I hope that the next time you begin to doubt yourself, you'll look back at our ride together through the pages of this book and understand that the power is in your hands to create the individual life that suits you best.

—Sifu William Moy

SPECIAL THANKS

The authors would like to extend their special thanks to these wonderful and talented individuals whose help was greatly appreciated on this project:

Sammo Hung
Mina Hung
Gine Lui
Russ Makofsky
Stacey Korolkova
Tak Wah Eng
Tish Das
Anthony Lucic
Karen Sheperd
Steven Cheung
Stan Kupchenko
Wendy Behar
Sifu Leo Imamura
Dr. Alberto Cayton
Myron Young
Sifu Henry Moy
Sifu Miguel
   Hernandez

Mark Elliston
Sifu Rex Aperauch
April Volponi
Dave Cowens
Sabrina Volponi
Frank Lovato
Christopher Grallert
Chris Fiali
Sifu Julie Ann
Denis Josselin
Sifu John Tsang
Kayla Harrison
Ila Borders
Doc-Fai Wong
Prof. Kevin Kennedy
Greg Ardon
Kayla Greenberg
Prof. Ellen Bialystok

Sifu Mickey Chan
Susan McGreevy-
   Nichols
Sifu Pete Pajil
Prof. Michelle
   LeBaron
Lea Page
Joel Wapnick
Sifu Tony Watts
Shaun Ledford
Al Perri
Josh Castro
Joseph Turcic